WITH SIGHS TOO DEEP FOR WORDS

GRACE AND DEPRESSION

A. ROBERT HIRSCHFELD

CHURCH
PUBLISHING
INCORPORATED

Unless otherwise noted, the Scripture quotations are from New Revised Standard Version Bible, copyright © 1989 National Council of the Churches of Christ in the United States of America. Used by permission. All rights reserved worldwide.

Page 94: "Prayer" from THE PAST by Galway Kinnell. Copyright © 1985 by Galway Kinnell. Reprinted by permission of Houghton Mifflin Harcourt Publishing Company. All rights reserved.

Church Publishing
19 East 34th Street
New York, NY 10016
www.churchpublishing.org

Cover design by Marc Whitaker, MTWdesign
Typeset by PerfecType Design, Nashville, Tennessee

Library of Congress Cataloging-in-Publication Data
Names: Hirschfeld, A. Robert, author.
Title: With sighs too deep for words : grace and depression / A. Robert
   Hirschfeld.
Identifiers: LCCN 2019056064 (print) | LCCN 2019056065 (ebook) | ISBN
   9781640652606 (paperback) | ISBN 9781640652613 (epub)
Subjects: LCSH: Depression, Mental--Religious aspects--Christianity. |
   Depressed persons--Religious life. | Joy--Religious
   aspects--Christianity.
Classification: LCC BV4910.34 .H57 2020   (print) | LCC BV4910.34
(ebook) |
   DDC 248.8/625--dc23
LC record available at https://lccn.loc.gov/2019056064
LC ebook record available at https://lccn.loc.gov/2019056065

To all the saints still striving,
and to all the saints at rest.

CONTENTS

CHAPTER ONE

DEPRESSION
AND JOY

The stigma of having any kind of mental illness has made me, like countless others, do my best to hide the fact that I live with depression. I can't help but wonder how those I admire, respect, love, and serve as a bishop think of me when I tell them I need to visit a therapist and that I live with a propensity for depression. Will they ascribe decisions or statements or positions I have taken, or mistakes I have made in my leadership and pastoral care, to a compromised mental state? No doubt, that possibility always exists, though perhaps not as much as I often fear. More likely, people who disagree or take issue with the ways I have been an ordained minister and leader in the church have plenty of other reasons to complain. They may disagree with the way I approach scripture or how I exercise episcopal authority. Thus far, at least, it has not been depression that might lead my sibling Christians to ask if the vocation I now inhabit is the right fit. Apart from me, it has only been Rocky, our black dog, who has questioned me openly about whether this bishop thing is of God or of someone or something else. And Rocky does that by staring intently at me with sighs too deep for words when I don't feel like throwing a stick in the backyard.

The truth is I am living with depression. And the emphasis is on the *living* with depression. Though almost every cell of my mind and body tells me not to share this truth with anyone, I have come to be convinced of the value of sharing this truth about myself with anyone who may find themselves in a similar state. We tell our stories because almost as soon as the words come out of our mouth we see a nod of the head, a softening of the eyes, a relaxing of the tension in the space between us. Our stories show others who we are, and virtually every time I have chosen to share something of my own struggle with someone who is herself burdened, it has been received as a lightening of that weight. For me, these liftings of the load of suffering are tangible evidence of the truth of the Gospel. John the Evangelist opens his gospel with:

> In the beginning was the Word, and the Word was with God, and the Word was God. . . . All things came into being through him, and without him not

one thing came into being. What has come into being in him was life, and the life was the light of all people. The light shines in the darkness, and the darkness did not overcome it.

John 1:1–5

I interpret the original Greek, *logos,* in a more fulsome way than merely "word." It could also be heard as "story" or "narrative." When I hear your story, and receive it in my heart, a connection is established that inevitably changes me and, I believe, changes you. The en-flesh-ment of God is how God's own story inhabits our own, and our own stories are brought back to God. When you and I share the narratives of our pains and struggles, our joys, accomplishments, and failures, we are, whether we acknowledge it or not, participating in the ongoing incarnating, suffering, resurrecting, and ascending work of God. In the telling of our stories, our own *logos,* God sends light upon us. Quite often, the light is just a flicker, a pinpoint, in the vast void. I have come to see in those meager piercings of the veil enough to hold on. They have been sufficient to teach me how *to live* with this disease.

Sometimes the light shining in the darkness takes the form of metaphor or images that catch the eye of my soul. Parables are literally disparate and unlike things "thrown together" to create new meaning. A treasure discovered in a field thrown together with the Realm of God. A mustard seed and the Realm of God. Who would think that those "throwing togethers" of Jesus have such world-changing power? And yet, we tell those stories continually because we crave to have our imaginations shaped by them and to see this world with the same heart-sight of Jesus. The sheer volume of Jesus's parables seems to me to give us permission to see our own parables. Here is one that I often see that gives me hope in God's healing.

In the woods behind our home stands a row of sugar maples that grow along an abandoned knee-high stone wall. The wall and trees probably formed a boundary for a pasture now overrun with new-growth hardwoods and hemlock. There are also rusty vestiges of a string of barbed wire, now broken and detached from the rotted cedar fence posts.

I occasionally visit one particular sugar maple that has grown around the barbed wire that once rubbed against its bark, such that the wire is now embedded in the tree. Some farmer thought of the tree as a conveniently planted post; over time the maple incorporated the steel barb into its heartwood. The wire is broken and detached on each side of the tree, but the life force of the tree, flowing from root to leaf and back again, has proven more resilient than the wound of those rusted barbs.

The tree tells me, every time I pass by it, that it is possible to live, grow, and even flourish with the wounds of this life. When looking at this tree, I see also the Tree of Life on which our Lord was pierced. I see within me wounds that cause me such grief at times and that won't leave me.

They rest within me, like barbed wire, forcing me at times to be still and silent so as to avoid further pain. The tree has learned to live with its dis-ease. I am called to do the same.

I imagine that the sugar maple tree recognizes me when I visit. I often recognize similar pain in the faces of many I encounter in the church and in the world. I deeply hope that the sharing of my story offers a hint of recognition and compassion for those who are suffering. My prayer is that in these pages they can find some comfort in being recognized and then have more hope to keep walking.

Though this book will be about depression, specifically my own depression, I hope it is as much a book about joy. I have come to the knotty truth that my depression arises of the deep gloom that gathers when joy seems utterly absent. For me, joy and depression are closely tied. How would I feel the absence of joy unless I have experienced or have implanted within me a pining for gloom's opposite? Joy, even in my most dilapidated moments, has left its footprints, its aftertaste, its fragrance in the same way that a church sanctuary on Sunday evening—the loneliest hour of the week for those who live alone—still holds the linger of the morning's incense and the atmospheric evidence of morning prayers in the shafts of the setting sun through stained glass windows. Joy and melancholy seem to be mysteriously, even brutally, entwined.

The Romantic poet John Keats suggested in the "Ode on Melancholy" that those who experience melancholy are those who recognize and treasure beauty and joy, especially in their departure.

> She dwells with Beauty—Beauty that must die;
>   And Joy, whose hand is ever at his lips
> Bidding adieu; and aching Pleasure nigh,
>   Turning to poison while the bee-mouth sips:
> Ay, in the very temple of Delight
>   Veil'd Melancholy has her sovran shrine,
>   Though seen of none save him whose
>   strenuous tongue
>   Can burst Joy's grape against his palate fine . . .

Though there is not a direct correspondence between the now mostly obsolete usage of "melancholy" and what we name as clinical depression, it seems fitting to say that depression lives in the debris of the desertions of joy and beauty.

Though what I share in this book is my own experience, I have worked hard not to universalize my history with mental illness; however, poets, writers, theologians, and commentators more gifted than I have left hints that those of us fighting in the trenches of depression share some of the same shape, stench, and muck. I am convinced that the cord that entwines both joy and suffering is the same tether that binds me to God. Some may read that statement as a naive leap. I get that. For many, the pain of depression is unmitigated hell, an inferno of destruction with no golden thread or silver lining.

Still, my depression continues to teach me about God's love and grace. I write, therefore, in the shaky hope that my experience might resonate with others who bear similar pain and struggle. My intent is to offer some hope to those who experience depression, especially those who have swallowed the dangerous myth that mental illness is somehow a moral flaw, or a sign of God's judgment, a myth that is tempting to believe—or at least has been for me.

As a bishop in the Episcopal Church, I have noticed more attention being paid to the "teaching office" of the episcopate: not only the expectation that bishops provide for the administration of the sacraments, stir the conscience of our people, and take part in the councils of the church, but also that we teach, which implies sharing what we have learned. My depression has forced me to learn things about myself, about the fragility of being human; about cruelty, forgiveness, compassion, resiliency, the power of prayer; about the Bible, about God and God's fierce tenderness; and about paradox and oxymorons such as fierce tenderness, invulnerable vulnerability, and the fear of God, which is the beginning of wisdom.

As both a parish priest and a bishop, I have been startled by the liberating power of sharing stories. When I have shared my own accounts of depression in small clergy gatherings, or in table conversation with my colleague bishops, there is almost universal resonance. People are given permission to share their own stories, however tentatively at first. With that sharing comes some shifting, some lightening, some easing of a burden that had been carried alone, convincing proof of some of Jesus's comforting words:

> Come to me, all you that are weary and are carrying
> heavy burdens, and I will give you rest. Take my
> yoke upon you, and learn from me; for I am gentle
> and humble in heart, and you will find rest for your
> souls. For my yoke is easy, and my burden is light.
>
> Matthew 11:28–30

A yoke is a double-looped device that allows two oxen or beasts of burden to share a load, making it easier on both of them. When I have shared my burden, and heard others share their pain from carrying the iron load of depression, I have felt the *comfort*—literally, the "with or together strength"—of God in Christ whose love is stronger than all our afflictions, even death itself.

FOR REFLECTION AND CONVERSATION

1. What keeps you from sharing your story—your pain—with others?
2. What are the primary parables or metaphors that are helpful to you?

3. Who can you talk to about your pain and struggle?
4. Who needs you to listen?

PRAYER

Our God and Source of all that is, in You we live, move, have our being: help me know you are close, even closer than I know myself. In our sighs, in our yearnings, in our pain, and in our confusion, hold me so that I can hold on when I feel lost, overwhelmed, and unable to find words. May my search for words find its end in You, the Word made flesh, through our Savior Jesus Christ. Amen.

CHAPTER TWO

A PECULIAR
KIND OF PAIN

It causes me some strain to describe what depression
feels like. All I can do is speak of my own experience
since I cannot get into the mind or fully know the activ-
ity of anyone else's brain. That being said, the literature
that speaks of states of mind and spirit, from the Book of
Psalms to more recent courageous accounts of those who
have been open about their own sensation of not being in
a right mind, all seem to share something that I understand as well: depression is painful, and it is a pain of a
different order. When I injured my neck in a football accident as a young teenager, the razor-like bolts that pulsed
down my arms and rendered them immobile was undeniable. All I could do—even though I remember somehow
walking to my parents' station wagon for the ride to the
emergency room—was feel pain, a knifing sharpness that

stung my shoulders, encased my scalp, and traveled down my left arm to my fingertips. At the hospital, there was no more walking or moving; the neurologists realized that any movement at all could have resulted in permanent damage and even paralysis.

The pain of my depression can be equally immobilizing, though mental illness is devious because usually I can still walk around without any obvious external sign of my internal suffering. There is nothing evident, like a hemorrhage or the protruding jagged edge of a fractured bone. At times, I am able to tell myself that maybe I am not living with a kind of pain at all. It's all in my head. I should be able to carry on as though nothing is happening, as though my power to function in the world is not compromised, as though there is not some viscous slurry inhibiting the sparking arcs of electrical charge that would otherwise glow among the cells of a healthy brain. I can hide my pain from both myself and others. It's perhaps not an accident that another word for skin is "hide." It is quite possible to conceal and suppress the effects of mental distress.

That being said, at the worst periods in my struggle I can physically feel psychological pain. It can arrive as a tingling in the scalp that makes even the roots of my hair want to just jump ship. Once, decades ago, I actually found clumps of hair clogging the shower drain. Food loses its flavor. The prospect of any physical contact makes my skin crawl. I want to avoid even a handshake. A hug, even from a loved one, triggers a wince. Lying next to my spouse in bed provides no comfort, and instead feels like a hostile invasion. The insidious nature of depression twists the suggestion of intimacy of any kind—physical or emotional or social—into a possible assault on my most vulnerable and delicate sense of safety and personhood, which may help to explain why one of the symptoms of depression is irritability: short-temperedness. An invitation to sit close on the couch, or to enjoy a dinner with friends, or to pick up a glove and play catch—all innocuous expectations of a spouse, friend, or child—are perceived as threats because all I want to do is sit alone in a room, perhaps with a book but usually not.

Sometimes depression feels like a heaviness behind my eyes, like a need, an urging, to cry, but there are no tears. A tantalizing in reverse. Perhaps it's hard to imagine a desire to weep, yet my depression sometimes makes me want to shed tears in the hope that something of my inner pain would be released through my tear ducts and I could wipe it away with a tissue. But no such luck. Instead the mysterious pain sits within me, immovable and obstinate.

In the woods of New England are rocks called "glacial erratics," massive prehistoric boulders that just stand there, alone among the trees and the hiking paths forced to detour around them. The giant rocks are remnants of the glacial age when the ice packs blanketing much of the earth receded and left behind their scrapings from the planet's surface. My depression feels like the same adamant presence in my head, sitting on top of fertile humus that would teem with life and growth if only the giant granite weight could somehow dissolve.

I suppose the lexicon of depression is vast because no simile or metaphor successfully captures the whole of it. What feels like an unyielding weight to one person may be a suffocating shadow to another. The novelist William Styron's classic memoir of depression, *Darkness Visible*, borrows its title from John Milton's poem *Paradise Lost*. That epic describes the fall of Adam and Eve, and the descent of angels from heaven who find themselves in a hell with flames that emit no light. It's a horrible scene, as the fallen find themselves consigned to a place

> As one great furnace flamed, yet from those flames
> No light, but rather darkness visible
> Served only to discover sights of woe,
> Regions of sorrow, doleful shades, where peace
> And rest can never dwell, hope never comes
> That comes to all . . .
>
> Book I, lines 62–67

A place without peace, scorching without light, visions of more woe, sad but without the subtle satisfaction of tears. Depression can be protean, constantly shifting in its shape to the sufferer, which is what makes it so damn difficult to engage.

We look for words to help us to contain, mold, shape— to get a handhold on—the chaos of existence, and depression is a phenomenon that seems infinitely able to defy description. It's not a fair fight.

We know what a paper cut or a sprained elbow or a stomachache feels like. There's a measure of satisfaction, though admittedly small, in being able to point to something and say, "My back aches," or "My headache pounds," "This pain is dull," or "That needle is sharp." Depression does not easily grant a correspondence between experience and language. Bianca, a fellow sufferer, describes her depression as "nonsensical pain. It's so shapeless and cloudy. It dodges all language." This makes it a particularly cruel condition to live with if your stock and trade are words.

Preachers, writers, journalists, teachers all have to speak. We carve sentences out of the raw lumber of our learning and experience to help others carve out a shape of their meaning, even if it's not a meaning they may find pleasant. And yet, mental illness is an area of life closely entwined with our being that remains ineffable, mysterious, beyond our capacity to articulate and share even with our closest companions.

The failure of language to embody the truth of mental illness has led me, among others, to feelings of alienation, loneliness, and dismal failure—feelings that only circle back and feed depression's voracious appetite. This vicious feedback loop supports the theory that depression is kin to aggression or anger turned inward. I hurt. Then I feel judged or shame for my pain. Unable to reason out of my pain, or to fully explain the shape of my particular hurt, I feel like a failure, so I hurt some more. On and on it goes. To be caught in this cycle feels imprisoning, without hope of release, which explains one of depression's hallmark symptoms: thoughts of suicide.

I have, at times, heard the inner distorting voices that would have me harm myself and even end my life. My compassion and feelings of grief toward those who have completed suicide grows deeper by the day. It is an act taken by a broken will. I cannot condemn or limit God's love toward the one who has made that choice, no matter how I might object or grieve. I have survived its siren call. The voices are real and undeniable. They have surprised me, coming at me when nothing in my personal, emotional, professional, or family life indicated that I was vulnerable to their attack. They have been shrieks sometimes, or dull moans—so unpredictable.

They have made me ever vigilant in my deliberate daily practices of prayer and self-care. I have been saved by intentionally reciting the Daily Office, and by the chance opening of the Book of Psalms. I have also been saved by summoning all of my strength simply to make my bed or brush my teeth, even talking to my toothbrush at the sink (as my wife once heard me), "You do this. And I will do this." Another day begun by noticing the most trivial, seemingly meaningless encounter with the things of this world and receiving them as life preservers.

If the prevalence of suicide in our society evokes outrage in me, it is because of our nation's paltry response to it. More American lives are lost to suicide every year than perished in the entire Vietnam conflict. Over 45,000 die by suicide annually. That's 110 lives *every day.* Yet there is no congressional commission charged with investigating the causes, no memorial on our National Mall, no monuments on our town squares.

The rationale for the absence of such markers is perhaps conceivable: society would rather not elevate or appear to celebrate such deaths, as though public acknowledgment would imply permission or even endorsement of the act. Traditional Christian moral reasoning has condemned suicide as a mortal sin warranting eternal damnation. In *The Divine Comedy*, Dante consigns suicides to the Seventh Circle of the Inferno where their souls are encased in trees whose branches continually sprout and then are broken off by tormenting harpies. It's a kind of damnation that does not portray so much their punishment but, strangely, the condition of despair that would actually lead a person to end their own agony. Dante seems to appeal to the reader's sympathy and compassion. It is not malice or hatred that leads the suffering souls to sever their bond with their bodies in death, but a desperate need to end their pain by dying.

We would do well to change our language when speaking of those whose death has come this way. A mother of a young man whose life ended this way gently and helpfully informed me that when we use the term "commit suicide" we make an equivalency with a crime. As a result, I now am more careful about my language and speak of those who have "ended their own lives" rather than those who have "committed" suicide. We want to make every possible moral, emotional, and spiritual appeal to dissuade someone from suicide, for their own sake and for the community of loved ones who are left behind, but tacking on the label of a crime is surely not helpful. The epidemic of suicide is made more insidious by our silence and our refusal to look at the persistent stigma of mental illness, which only enforces the isolation of its sufferers. People are most often dissuaded from attempting suicide because someone makes contact with them and reminds them they are not alone. A simple request—"Promise you will call me if you think you are going to hurt yourself"—can be life-giving.

To be a Christian minister who lives with depression often feels like a strange and peculiar phenomenon to me. I feel like in my preaching, public witness, teaching, and diocesan administration I am expected to point to the joy and hope Jesus promises us. And I work to do that. I do not believe my depression is worsened by doing the work of ministry, nor that my ministry is devalued by my depression. It is, as I said, a peculiar kind of pain. In many ways I have supports that so many others do not. I can call friends and colleagues who know and share the particular stresses of ordained ministry. The health insurance offered through the Church Pension Group provides exceptional service, especially if one needs to find therapists and mental health care providers. And, I have learned, I can speak honestly—from the pulpit, on the page, and in person—about what it feels like to live with depression, which reminds me I am not alone.

To say that depression is a peculiar kind of pain is not to say that it is unique. The big lie of depression is that I am the only one who feels as I do. That breeds the isolation and despair that can lead to suicide. And it is a lie. I am not alone, either in my feelings or in my struggle. You are not alone. Others feel the same way. Others love us and want to help, want to listen. We do not have to face this by ourselves.

For Reflection and Conversation

1. Have you had times when you have contemplated harming yourself? What did you do?
2. What resources do you have to deal with those times?

PRAYER

O God, you are in both the light and the shadow, you are there even when we are desolate and utterly convinced of your absence: find us when we are lost. Be especially with those who now are at a close risk of harming themselves or even of dying by their own hand. Put far from them the means of ending their lives. O God of infinite love and compassion, please receive in tenderness the souls of those who have died by suicide, and show signs of your gentle presence to those who have survived an attempt and to their loved ones. Help us all hold on to your promise of life. Grant us the light of hope when our minds are shrouded in despair. In the name of Jesus, whose love and presence with us is stronger than death. Amen.

CHAPTER THREE

MYSTERY

If I have gained any certainty about factors that are responsible for a person being depressed, it is in the word "mystery." Physicians, pharmacological experts, therapists, fellow sufferers of depression, and religious leaders all wander in the land of mystery when it comes to explaining what is going on in the brain to cause it to be depressed. Some argue that one is disposed to the illness as a result of how one is born into the world. In our age of genetic mapping, we have looked for a gene, or several genes, that are coded for depression, just as genes determine whether one is brown-eyed or left-handed. Others look for explanation in our nurture—external influences, experiences, trauma, and history. Some use the metaphorical language of a moral or spiritual battle. Some say depression may be the effect of sin, either one's own or that inflicted by another.

Our faith both explains and relieves our suffering, even as it leaves things unexplained and unsettled. An acquaintance who clearly has his doubts about the value of psychotherapy given the marked rise in depression, anxiety, and suicide wrote in an e-mail, "God, not couches!" I was tempted to offer a somewhat flippant response, "God so often talks to me when I'm on the couch." But flippant responses to e-mails usually lead me down a path of deeper annoyance. Still, faith and therapy are not mutually exclusive.

The field of epigenetics suggests that our spiritual, environmental, and inherited traits are all woven together at a cellular level. The damaging effect of trauma can actually alter our chromosomes and even be passed to the generation that follows. In other words, I may have inherited something of my ancestors' response to violence they witnessed or experienced. We can only begin to imagine the lingering and powerful damage of war, environmental degradation or disaster, and mass incarceration that has been visited upon generations and generations of God's children. At this writing, our nation is confronting scenes of children living in the awful squalor of detention camps that concentrate the effects of human brutality. If and when these children are released and returned to their families, the effects of their experiences in detention will endure well into their adulthood, and also be passed on to their descendants.

We might hear the Bible's own "epigenetic" understanding of sin in Exodus when Moses receives the two tablets of stone upon which are etched the Ten Commandments. The effect of sin is resilient as it passes from one generation to another.

> The LORD, the LORD, a God merciful and gracious, slow to anger, and abounding in steadfast love and faithfulness, keeping steadfast love for the thousandth generation, forgiving iniquity and transgression and sin, yet by no means clearing the guilty, but visiting the iniquity of the parents upon the children and the children's children, to the third and the fourth generation.
>
> Exodus 34:6–7

I have always been troubled by those verses and the statement that the sins of one generation will not only apply to those who initially disobey the law, but will extend even beyond their great-great-grandchildren. God help us.

Though it is difficult to accept the notion of inherited consequences for the sins of our ancestors, modern medicine resonates with the Bible in understanding that each generation does inherit the habits of the mind, the culture, the ecological health or disease, the racial and class inequities, and the international conflicts and tensions that began well before that generation was born. The racial disparities of our school systems and housing and access to capital are not realities we created. We inherited them. We have also inherited the way our culture is addicted to our unfettered freedom to drive a multiton gas-powered automobile when it is a phenomenon only a little more than a century old, and despite its having contributed massively to our current environmental crises. The lingering and enduring consequences of any number of things can certainly feel like chastisement, punishment.

Living with depression can feel the same way. Yet, I take heart that I stand in the same steadfast love of God that Moses encountered on the holy mountain, as passionate and fiery as that love is. I find some comfort in the biblical word translated as "fear," as in "the fear of the LORD is the beginning of wisdom" (Ps. 111:10). Such fear is not terror but reverence. It is a deep feeling that has accompanied me my whole life, as much a part of my soul and spirit as my deepest hope. I believe my depression has taught me that the fear of the Lord's infinite love and agency in my life—a sense that it is beyond my control and my understanding—is part of what binds me close to God's heart. It's not something I would ask any therapist or spiritual director to assuage or erase.

Quite often we want to say that depression can be more simply explained by an imbalance of chemicals in the brain. The multi-billion-dollar pharmaceutical industry has done its level best to convince us that happiness and joy are to be found in the optimal equilibrium of chemicals, enzymes, and hormones as they interact with the densely complex assortment of biological wires called neurons within our skulls. As almost any doctor will tell you, there is nothing simple or uncomplicated about the chemical and electric composition of the brain's proper functioning.

That said, I have benefited from antidepressants for the vast majority of my years as a parish priest. Prozac, Zoloft, Wellbutrin, and Celexa have all been companions on my walk with Jesus. I have had an often conflicted and confusing history with them, and have become reconciled in my relationship to them over the years. I list these pharmaceuticals to underscore just how complicated my own brain's chemistry has proven to my physicians and psychiatrist.

There have been periods when I have felt sufficiently strong and self-sustaining that I seriously questioned why I was taking the meds. My inner arguments began, "If you were really healthy, if you really believed in the joy of Christ, you wouldn't need to take this little pill every morning. Who else do you know in your position who needs this little helper? Why not get off it and see what happens? Wouldn't it be grand if you were free of all external aids that make you who you are?" I then consulted with my psychiatrist, and he agreed to experiment with tapering off the medication. This occurred maybe twice in our twenty-plus-year relationship. Both times I realized that living without the antidepressants brings on a nocuous mix of gloom, nausea, irritability, and fear, and I was relieved to restablish my dosage so I could function. This is an experiment I intend not to repeat.

As it turns out, I am part of the human race. If I were to have another condition, one not so attached to the cultural or religious stigma as mental illness, would I feel so judged for taking my medicine? The pain of gout is so acute and unbearable, so debilitating to me when I am suffering an attack, that I can be of little help or comfort or kindness to those around me. Why would I not take Allopurinol, which keeps me from having my foot amputated? If I lived with asthma, who would fault me for using treatments or medications that would allow me to breathe?

If I could wave a magic wand, I would love to remove the societal baggage that can hinder me and so many others from accepting help for mental illness. How I wish I could silence the voice that I can still hear within myself and from others that says, "If you were only stronger, more resilient, you wouldn't need the assistance of therapy, counseling, medication, or a hospital. Why can't you just get over it?" These shadow remarks, of course, only have the effect of leading us down tunnels of deeper alienation and distress. What a comfort it was once when, while staying with longtime family friends for an overnight visit, I heard my chum enter the kitchen and announce that he was ready to join our breakfast "because I just had my morning toilet, shaved, and have taken my antidepressant!"

There is freedom, joy, and life in welcoming ourselves to the human race.

I take my antidepressants because they help me live with my depression. As an ordained religious leader, I stridently counsel those who find themselves wondering if they should take their medication or follow their doctor's orders, "Take your medication! Please." Do not decide to change or abstain from your prescribed dosage on your own. In the name of the God who has blessed scientists and those involved in the healing arts to discover these therapies, take your medicine.

Recent research has now almost irrefutably proven that there is also a genetic component to depression. Trauma experienced generations ago in one of my ancestors may have altered the genetic material passed on to me, even as "I was knit together in my mother's womb" (Ps. 139:13). Here, science resonates with statements in the Bible about the effect of sin being passed on from generation to generation. Though that may at first seem a demoralizing thought— how can I beat something that lives in my genes?—I am convinced, even if I don't always understand, that God's grace and presence as communicated by talk therapy, pharmaceuticals, or more intense treatments changes the genes I will pass along. The explanation of the actual mechanics of these therapies eludes scientists, theologians, and me. There is still plenty of room for mystery.

Depression is often fed by circumstance. Climate change. Overpopulation. Our torn social fabric. The intractability of our strained conversations around race, gender, and class. The epidemic of gun violence. The epidemic of suicide. Life is depressing, and our societal depression often seems to border on despair.

How, then, do you and I cope with the circumstances of life when our individual actions don't appear to make much of a difference? How can we reverse the effects of hundreds of years of industrial and cultural dependence on fossil fuels, toxic chemicals and plastics, poor stewardship of water and air, and extraction of flora and fauna that have led to irreversible damage to our planet? How do we reconcile our hope to be "good, loving, faithful Christians" when other "good, loving, faithful Christians" have not only justified these practices but amplified their destruction by wounding their fellow human beings through slavery and other forms of oppression?

I am almost paralyzed to write anything after that seemingly hopeless paragraph. And that's where depression, whether clinical or circumstantial—caused by racial discord or ecological grief or trauma—would have us stay: paralyzed, incapacitated, and stuck in despair without any sense of mystery or community. One of the big lies of depression is isolation: I am on my own; no one feels as I feel.

We did not get into these horrible predicaments alone, despite the popular individualistic, Lone Ranger understanding of ourselves. Neither will we get out of these traps on our own. If there will be an effective response that rises to the enormity of the damage caused to the great web of relationships that bind us to each other, to God, and to God's creation, it will be in learning—again—that we are interwoven. Together, we are woven into a web of being that reflects the love that flows among the Three Persons of the Trinity in whose image we are created.

The Gospels often tell us that when Jesus saw hungry crowds or an afflicted person, he had compassion for them. The English word "compassion" means "suffer with." It is not a condescending pity, but a deep and visceral empathy. The Greek word literally means "intestinal": a gusty kind of love. It shares the same root as the word "spleen"—the organ that does so much to keep our blood healthy. The English word "splenetic" is defined as a predisposition to being angry, irascible, and melancholy. Depression and compassion, it seems, come from the core of our beings, one drawing us into isolation and the other into relationship. Our pain can pull us into despair or bind us together in community. Another mystery.

The German word *Weltschmerz* means "world pain"— the pain felt not only by humankind, but by the planet itself. Depression may not only be a sign of a disorder of the brain, but also of a brain that is awake to reality in the same way that post-traumatic stress disorder is no longer thought of in only pathological terms but as a natural and predictable response to the actual disorders of war, abuse, violence, and moral injury. A friend who witnessed first-hand horrors of war that he finds painfully difficult to recount once told me that, though he is grateful that the listing in the *Diagnostic and Statistical Manual of Mental Disorders (DSM-5)* has brought greater public sympathy and respect to those who are so diagnosed, he laments the word "disorder" in the diagnosis. War is the disorder, he says. The human response to it is not disordered at all, but a natural and logical reaction to incomprehensible violence experienced in such closeness.

We don't know everything that causes depression. We don't know when the wars will end. We don't know how long we have. We don't know how to fix the systems that oppress so many. We don't know what will happen next. Not knowing can be frightening, but fear is not assuaged by certainty. Love drives away fear. Hope grows in mystery. In all that we don't know, there is room for mystery.

FOR REFLECTION AND CONVERSATION

1. What are some of the things that inspire you or give you a sense of mystery or awe?
2. How have you dealt with the inherited consequences of your family of origin?
3. What do you think and how do you feel about taking antidepressants?

4. When have you been welcomed to the human race and felt accepted for being who you are, in whatever condition you are?
5. How do we help one another choose relationship over isolation?

PRAYER

O Lord Jesus, you met people of all conditions, and you loved them. Oftentimes we feel we need to be better, more whole, more happy, more together, just more than we really are. Free us from the need to keep up false appearances, which are so exhausting to maintain. Meet us and touch us in whatever space or condition we find ourselves, and give us the courage we need to accept the help you extend to us through the healing arts. In your strong name we pray. Amen.

CHAPTER FOUR

WAITING FOR THE
BEAUTY OF THE RUINS

My depression has a complicated and contradictory effect on my senses. On the one hand, I can feel hyperaware of everything around me. The struggle of a hummingbird trapped in the garage, wings whirring against the impervious glass, can plunge me into a consuming dread as I fight to find a way to usher her out. On the other hand, a terrorist act that leaves scores dead at a wedding in Afghanistan deadens my nerves and I become so glum as to feel almost apathetic, as though my soul, like a drenched sponge, cannot absorb any more. Everything in life, both small and great, is too much to bear. In those moments, the temptation to leave in the most drastic way I can leave—by ending my life—is acute and real.

The late Galway Kinnell wrote a poem called "Wait" to a student whose heartbreak led her to contemplate suicide. It's a poem I have prescribed to more than a few anguished souls in my years of ministry because it has soothed my own barbed mind on countless occasions. Kinnell faces despair by leaning into the wisdom of the ancients: wait.

A more liturgical phrasing for "wait" is "keep vigil." One of my life preservers has been the practice of keeping vigil, of waiting for the shroud of gloom to dissolve and for things to recover to a level in the universe that I can tolerate. More accurately, what I keep vigil for is my capacity to engage reality without being debilitatingly overwhelmed. This practice of moderating my intake of the hardness of life is one I share with others who live with depression and other kinds of mental illness. Some are very careful not to watch television or listen to news reports. Monitoring our engagement with visual and auditory violence and hatred, so rampant in our day, might be construed as being aloof, detached, or unconcerned. To the contrary, I have found practices like deactivating Facebook or Twitter accounts, not watching the evening news, and instead getting news from print media (which can be picked up or put down as needed) are acts of care for the soul.

Wait. Keep vigil. Stay still. Breathe. Be.

I have learned to be more willing to wait for the return of a kind of enchantment in the ordinary things of life. Depression can certainly dull the senses and foment perpetual disinterest in things both great and small. Wait for things that have become banal to become interesting again. Wait for the painful memories to be rejoined to a melody that sings of life with a kind of focused, exhausting purpose.

Kinnell ends his poem by calling us to wait until we can hear the music of our whole lives "rehearsed by the sorrows, play itself into total exhaustion." I hear the exhaustion in the way a child is exhausted after a day of playing tag or hide-and-seek with friends until it's dark. Or the way a couple is spent after lovemaking. Or the way one is tired after a good day tending the garden. That kind of exhaustion is good and holy. The exhaustion of the depressed, the mentally ill, the desolate, is of another sort.

Depression can dull my capacity to tell the difference. There are times when the world feels so vacated of purpose and meaning that the mind and body get stuck in immobility. The Psalmist refers to the "sickness that lays waste at mid-day," from which Andrew Solomon derived the title of his exploration of depression, *The Noonday Demon: An Atlas of Depression.* As he recounts his own experiences of breakdowns and agony, he shares the poem of a friend, Elizabeth Prince, whose intense suffering causes her to withdraw from the world and even forces a wedge between herself and the most basic of bodily functions:

I was in my room, hiding,
hating the need to swallow.[1]

---

1. Andrew Solomon, *The Noonday Demon: An Atlas of Depression* (New York: Scribner, 2001), 54–55.

I am surprised by how depression affects the most unlikely of persons. Since junior high school I have admired the lyrical genius of Bruce Springsteen. I can remember sitting in the passenger seat of my parents' car, my hand on the dial of the FM radio. I drove everyone to utter annoyance as I kept spinning the dial back and forth until "Born to Run" poured out of the crackling speakers in our old Pontiac. Such exuberance. Such drive for life. Such passion. How could the same genius of verse, muscle, and guitar be laid low by depression? And yet Springsteen writes in his autobiography:

> Shortly after my sixtieth [birthday] I slipped into a depression like I hadn't experienced since that dusty night in Texas thirty years earlier. It lasted for a year and a half and devastated me. When these moods hit me, usually few will notice . . . but Patti [his spouse] will observe a freight train bearing down, loaded with nitroglycerin and running quickly out of track. . . . [D]eath I can handle; it's this other . . . *thing*. This thing I have studied and fought against for the better part of sixty-five years. It comes in darkness or in broad daylight, each time wearing a subtly different mask, so subtle that some like myself who have fought it and named it multiple times welcome it in like an old friend. Then

once again it takes up deep residence in my mind, heart and soul until it is finally routed out after doing its wreckage.[2]

Springsteen's description of his depression as a freight train full of nitroglycerin and running out of track takes me back to the time I cut my hand deeply while repairing one of my children's bicycles. A piece of white metal snapped and sliced into my palm, exposing flesh, muscle, and bone. At first there was no pain, as though my nerves needed time to react to the trauma. Then a slight movement of air across the gash awakened a stinging and singeing pain. Any touch—of air, of cloth, of water, of *anything*—triggered the pain.

My depression is like that, which makes me wonder if the impulse to stay in bed, not to move, not to budge or talk or hear any noise, or be touched by anything or anyone, is not because I am growing more numb, but because the pain is too intense to move.

When Galway Kinnell talks about waiting until things such as music, gloves, and hair become interesting again, I read the word "interesting" as alluding to something that becomes tolerable, curious, or fascinating in a way that does

---

2. Bruce Springsteen, *Born to Run* (New York: Simon & Schuster, 2016), 484–485.

not cause undue mental or spiritual anguish. German novelist Hermann Broch wrote, "Waiting is like barbed wire stretched inside one." The peculiar stinging within me when I am in the depths of depression is exacerbated by any kind of movement. Can I find any balm during such excruciating periods?

I have found that the word "wait" helps me because it reminds me of the long Christian tradition of keeping vigil, of spiritual waiting for God's kingdom. We wait in Advent. We wait in Lent. The repeated words of a Taizé chant offer some succor:

> Wait for the Lord,
> whose day is near.
> Wait for the Lord.
> Be strong.
> Take heart.

Alongside the metaphors of a train full of nitro, barbed wire, and open gashes lie the possible blessings that the hyper-tenderness of depression may have afforded me. I have had moments of possible vision, or epiphany, of divine disclosure that have accompanied my journey with this cursed condition.

To say so must come with a serious caveat: I am not visionary. I am hesitant to declare that the depressed mind is more imaginative, more creative, or more aesthetically or philosophically sensitive. We carry a cultural myth that those with mental illness tend to be more creative and artistic. Perhaps among the pool of artists are those who are more likely to suffer from bipolar disorder, depression, or schizophrenia. We frequently romanticize mental illness, as if to say that mental anguish is often the cost of being a creative genius.

I seriously doubt that my mental illness has brought me any closer to the gates of paradise or made me more creative. But having said that, there have been moments when I have felt convinced that God was showing up for me in a certain assuring way, as though to remind me of what my depression would have me quickly dismiss or forget: I am not alone; there is a Presence that loves, and loves *me*.

FOR REFLECTION AND CONVERSATION

1. The word "wait" can mean everything from waiting for a doctor's report to waiting for Christmas morning. What does waiting—keeping vigil—mean to you?

2. In this chapter, depression is described as exhaustion and as an explosive runaway train. How do you describe it?

3. What books, songs, and stories are helpful to you as you live with depression?

PRAYER

Fill me with a sense of your living, caring presence, O God, especially when I feel you are so far and that I am incapable of feeling joy again. If I cannot feel joy, help me be satisfied for this moment and the next in the memory of knowing your joy. Help me be still and know that you are God, and that to be able to even address you is sufficient for this hour and the next. Help me be satisfied with this moment in your presence. Keep me. Hold me. Amen.

CHAPTER FIVE

A RUIN IN THE WOODS

I surmise that living with depression makes me more sensitive to the spaces in which I live and move and have my being. When under the pall of a depressive episode, I can become more defenseless to the effects of sound or sight, or even a particular atmosphere or the air of a place. Certain combinations of objects, slants of light, as the poet Emily Dickinson noticed, can seize and demand my attention. It is as though reality takes on a different quality, an aura begotten in spiritual anguish. Not quite hallucination—what I see and feel is actually *there* and seen by others. But *what* is there takes on a kind of super reality, a gloss of truth that is more heightened, more intense. When Jesus gave a blind man sight in Mark's gospel, there is a moment when it seems there are two kinds of seeing: what is there, and what is perhaps even more there.

[Jesus] took the blind man by the hand and led him out of the village; and when he had put saliva on his eyes and laid his hands on him, he asked him, "Can you see anything?" And the man looked up and said, "I can see people, but they look like trees, walking." Then Jesus laid his hands on his eyes again; and he looked intently and his sight was restored, and he saw everything clearly. Then he sent him away to his home, saying, "Do not even go into the village."

Mark 8:23–26

Are the trees there? Are the people there? Are the trees like people? Can a tree be like a person or a person like a tree? When the mind is "broken," all the distinctions of ordinary existence sometimes seem, well, less distinctive and both blurred and intense. It's curious how the word translated as "looked intently" suggests a more intensified, penetrating vision. The unnamed man is now separated from his companions, urged by Jesus to "not even go into the village."

Seeing things differently from others can be isolating. I wonder why Jesus sends this newly sighted man home without even having him check in with his peers. I want to think that when he returns to his home it will be not to an empty house and that he will be surrounded by loved ones eager to rejoice and celebrate in his healing and his restored vision. It may be among such trusted ones that the anonymous man can explore what he saw when he was blind and what he now can see.

Soon after Jesus gives this man his vision, we are given another vision in the Transfiguration of Jesus on a mountain. There, Peter and James and John are taken with Jesus to pray and suddenly,

> he was transfigured before them, and his clothes became dazzling white, such as no one on earth could bleach them.
>
> Mark 9:2b–3

We know the Transfiguration as the quintessential "mountaintop" experience, one of those moments when there is no doubt of one's closeness to God and God's presence, loving and strong. We all hope for these moments and their echoes—falling in love, welcoming the birth of a child and relishing in a loved one's flourishing, finding ourselves reconciled with someone from whom we've previously been estranged, recovering from an illness or injury. So exhilarating are such moments that we might feel invulnerable to any suffering. The sun shines even if it's raining outside.

One symptom of depression is that the capacity for a "mountaintop" experience is broken or disabled. It is as though the capacity to see God's work and presence in the world, even the capacity to feel joy, is seriously damaged. I have noticed in myself, and in others who have disclosed their diagnosis of depression to me, that hardly any feeling of wonder, joy, sometimes even pain or compassion, can penetrate the protective shield that surrounds the heart. A yawning gulf widens between the self and what is real. And that hardly feels like living.

But then occasionally, unpredictably and without control, the carapace of my usual awareness breaks open, and I seem to see things like the man did whose eyelids were moistened with the spit of Jesus.

I remember walking in a large wooded area near our home in Western Massachusetts once and coming upon a vintage Volkswagen Beetle from the sixties. It was rusting in the forest, off an abandoned farm road that was bordered on one side by a stone wall. The driver's side door was broken off, and the passenger side door was pockmarked with bullet holes. A young oak tree, maybe twenty years old, had pushed up through the rear hollow where the engine once purred. Small pine trees were beginning to sprout from the wheel wells where humus and moss had collected over the years of decomposing leaves and rain.

The sight stopped me in my tracks. The scene of this derelict automobile seemed flooded with an aura of some numinous significance. I could not help but wonder what the Volkswagen abandoned in the forest *meant*. Perhaps a less needful and less anguished mind would have dismissed the scene as another example of our throwaway culture, or as a waste of a good, reliable car. They might have strolled on with a shrug.

But I felt the need to stop. I sat on a neighboring glacial rock and paid homage, as though it were the burning bush from which God might speak to me. If my depression has sensitized to such transfigurations where the mysterious and sacred is revealed in the corrupted and common, then I may have some cause to be grateful for my disorder and to appreciate that it allows me to see the hallowedness behind the pall of the ordinary.

It is worth learning how to wait, to keep vigil, for the moments when stones, bushes, and rusted jalopies speak.

Without doubt there is an exhilaration and delight in entering newly built or refurbished spaces. As a bishop I am occasionally asked to bless newly renovated sanctuaries or parish halls that had become tired or dilapidated. It's a privilege to share the joy and pride of wardens and building committees when they unveil to me old spaces made new or expanded for the use of the wider community. What could have fallen into ruin from neglect or carelessness were restored to uses that often signify how the congregations desire to dignify the users of these spaces. What had been drab, low-ceilinged, poorly lit parish halls that smelled stale and musty now are settings where twelve-step meetings, community suppers, after-school art or tutoring programs, and vestry meetings may somehow seem more exalted and noble because they take place in rooms where it is more evident that the congregation cares and wishes to honor those who enter its doors. I'm not talking about spaces that look like they may be depicted in a *Martha Stewart Living* or *Architectural Digest* magazine, but uncluttered and carefully finished places with simple furnishings, a fresh coat of paint, and simple, tasteful lighting. I'm thinking in particular of one such parish hall, which is located in a completely gutted early nineteenth-century house with nothing but the outer walls in place and all the original timber rafters, columns, and floor beams exposed. When I walk into that space to share Shrove Tuesday pancakes or take part in the summer art camp for local children, my spirit lifts with the height and light of the room.

But more often I am invited into undercrofts, cellars really, of churches where the carpet is musty and worn, the fluorescent lights above sputter, the plumber's putty that keeps the bathroom plumbing from leaking shows its age. The editors of *Martha Stewart Living* or *Town and Country* magazine would be going catatonic. Ruins.

But what such influencers of good taste probably can't see, but I can, is the quality of love in the room. The people have brought their best time-honored casseroles, some from recipes that came from generations past. The particular mix of aromas of coffee and wet wool and boots from the hunters, lumberjacks, and chairlift operators waft up into the fiberglass hung ceilings. There is clean laughter and cheerfulness, genuine welcome and embrace among the people who upstairs in the sanctuary prayed for their loved ones struggling with opioids, the lingering bodily injuries of car accidents, slips on the ice or down the stairs.

Here's the thing: I think my depression has knocked most of the snobbery out of me. If I ever believed that being an Episcopalian meant inhabiting a façade of "having it all together," with polished wing-tip shoes, a crisp crease in pin-striped trousers, and a shining silver or gold chain for my pectoral cross, I don't anymore. In fact, I soon became embarrassed by the shiny stuff of my office, preferring the crosier made from an ash tree that fell victim to a local insect infestation that is laying waste to almost every ash tree in northern New England, and a length of rawhide for the steel pectoral cross given me in memory of my deceased beloved sister.

There are things in this life that cause suffering and leave ruins. As Christians we live and move among them daily. My depression is partly the effect of past suffering that my brain and soul is still digesting, the way nature takes care of trees that have fallen and with time and weather converts the arbor's once majestic mass into soft, rich, black humus on a forest floor. Or the way an adorable old Volkswagen Beetle becomes a shot-up, corroded habitat for all sorts of living things near an abandoned farm road in the woods. My depression may be the result of things I've forgotten. It can also be the lens through which I have come to see the beauty, sometimes even the splendor, of being fully human in this catastrophic world.

FOR REFLECTION AND CONVERSATION

1. In what ways does depression set you apart from those closest to you?
2. Who makes up the community of friends or support that you rely on when you feel particularly alone and isolated?
3. What are the "ruins" of your life that give you meaning?
4. Where have you seen beauty or grace in places that the culture might consider ugly, unattractive, or without grace?

PRAYER

O Lord Jesus, you wept for Jerusalem, yearning to gather her children up into your arms like a mother hen broods over her young. You see my disasters, catastrophes, messes, and yet you come close to walk with me and to love me. Help me see my imperfections and failures, the ruins of my life and the world as a chance to draw near only to you. Show me signs of beauty and wonder where the world sees only corruption, decay, ruin. Shine your light upon me and all that I see, so that I behold you in all things. Amen.

CHAPTER SIX

The Practice of I AM

I wish I had some secret sauce, some special recipe, some powerful combination of methods, thoughts, techniques, or procedures that could provide relief to others who grapple with the noonday demon, the dark night of the soul, the black dog, the barbed wire stretched inside, the darkness visible, or whatever name describes their particular experience of depression. Though I am cautious about universalizing my own experience, I have noticed that my depression seems to bring me into proximity with others who know what I'm talking about.

Sometimes, I imagine that I am a priest who carries an invisible gremlin on his shoulder, invisible except to those who also carry a similar gremlin with them. We recognize each other by a look, or a tone of voice. They say that misery loves company. I'm not so sure. But it has occurred to me that depression, when it's out on the street, or in the workplace, or in the supermarket, seems to recognize itself in others. This is a good thing, though it could be a better thing if we knew how to more easily bridge the gaps between us. Practitioners of the twelve-step groups sometimes identify themselves with bumper stickers, jewelry, T-shirts, caps, even tattoos that indicate that they "take one day at a time," or that they are a "friend of Bill W," or that they "let go and let God." These public confessions hold both freedom and power. The freedom is in being able to share their vulnerability openly without feeling the pressure to keep up the appearances of being in control. The power is in realizing the strength that comes from companionship and collegiality, even among strangers. Depression, like addiction, gains devastating momentum when it makes us believe we are alone, isolated and cut off from others. The early church found freedom and power in *koinonia*—sharing, participation, communion, fellowship, community—the loving, liberating, and life-giving power of not being alone. The cruelty of depression, like many other diseases, is in its impulse to make one feel utterly isolated. And yet, we can see each other, even across the span of our isolation.

Over the next several chapters, I want to offer a few of the ways I have found to survive my own affliction, in the hope that there may be something that is useful for another. This, too, is recovery work, but not in the sense that we might one day fully recover from our mental illness. In my experience, and that of others I have been blessed to encounter, depression is never completely behind us.

Instead, we learn to live, fully and blessedly, in its mottled landscape.

The metaphor reminds me of a recent hike to a summit in the White Mountains where I looked at the neighboring peaks and the valley below. It was a clear day. The shadows of the scattered clouds danced across the lush green forest floor, creating several shades of green, some bright, some more somber. The variegation made the landscape more interesting. It called to my mind a familiar collect from the Book of Common Prayer:

> Grant us, Lord, not to be anxious about earthly things, but to love things heavenly; and even now, while we are placed among things that are passing away, to hold fast to those that shall endure; through Jesus Christ our Lord, who lives and reigns with you and the Holy Spirit, one God, for ever and ever.[3]

One of the ways I have found "to hold fast to those [things] that shall endure" is centering prayer. Obviously, I did not discover this method of prayer. It has been a practice among people and communities of many faiths for millennia. Contemporary proponents are Thomas Keating,

---

3. BCP, 234.

Eckhart Tolle, Cynthia Bourgeault, James Finley, Richard Rohr, and Julia Gatta.

The mid-1980s were an unsettled and swirling period of my life. In the midst of my first matriculation in seminary and the collapse of a young and frail marriage, I happened upon the presence of a contemplative whose teaching has helped to ground me through many subsequent tempests. Rachel Hosmer was an Episcopal priest, one of the first women to be ordained, founder of the Order of St. Helena, and a professor of spiritual theology at General Theological Seminary in New York. I don't remember how I found myself in her study one dreary February afternoon when I was about a hair's breadth from withdrawing from seminary and returning my certificate of postulancy to my bishop. Her presence both intimidated and calmed me; she told me to sit still and be quiet. She asked if I was comfortable in silence. When I answered yes, she said, "Not just quiet. But silence. How much time do you spend in silence?"

"Not much."

"Then let's."

She began to speak, quietly, about the word "*Eimi*" (pronounced A-ME). It's a word Jesus used a lot; it means "I am." Jesus hearkens back to the revelation of God to Moses in the burning bush. Moses asked who he should say had sent him to Pharaoh with the demand to free the Hebrew people. God uttered a name which was holier than any other: I AM WHO I AM; I WILL BE WHAT I WILL BE (Exodus 3:14).

Jesus said "I am" a number of times. I am the Good Shepherd. I am the door. I am the gatekeeper. I am the Bread of Life. I am the Light of the world. Or simply I AM, to the soldiers in the Garden of Gethsemane who had come to arrest him.

"You seem to be in tumult. God is here. And so are you. You are. God is. I am. That's all we have in the end. Silence is where we start. Silence is where we end." Mother Rachel then invited me to sit still and say, *Ego Eimi.* To repeat it several times out loud, and then to repeat it to myself in silence.

We sat there for another hour. For a few moments, interspersed between my awareness of the city outside, the occasional car horn or a name shouted from the sidewalk, I felt a presence. It was not constant. I had to forget the awkwardness of sitting alone in a simple room with a woman I had only met once or twice after chapel, the two hard-backed chairs and a few books, the simple cross on the cracked white wall.

Ego Eimi. I am.

I have taken frequent refuge in those words since then, almost daily. And always in the throes of a depressive episode. Sometimes I sit in an upright chair, my cell phone or laptop in another room. When I am more deeply "funked" I lie on a couch and close my eyes, placing my hands across my chest as though I'm in a casket. I don't know when that particular habit started, but it's comfortable and reminds me of Mother Rachel's words: "Silence is where we start. Silence is where we end."

Silence is the milieu of all authentic relationships, quite different from the jumpy "monkey mind" that finds my thoughts bouncing all over my to-do lists, my failures, my "woulda coulda shouldas," my comparisons with the accomplishments and acquisitions of others, all of which lead me deeper into the funk.

Ego Eimi. I am. I am.

The words are more than a mere affirmation of myself, as though I am the only one in the world who is important. It connects me to Jesus, the Jesus who seeks me, deep within me, deeper than my frail and faltering synapses that are clogged by my neural muck.

"Jesus," I pray, "point me to the I AM who is and who is of the God who wants to create me anew, even out of the muck that has my wheels stuck and spinning, even out of the tomb of my depression."

After a time, I stand up. I rise, renewed, however incrementally.

FOR REFLECTION AND CONVERSATION

1. What does it mean to you to think of God as I AM or another form of the verb TO BE?

2. What does it mean to you to be created in the image of God?

3. How have you found silence to be meaningful?
4. How have you found silence to be difficult?

PRAYER

Help. Me. Be.
Help. Me.
Help.
Be.
Amen.

CHAPTER SEVEN

MOVING THE IMMOVABLE

I've referred to depression as an immovable "glacial erratic," a huge boulder left behind by a receding glacier that has scraped and carved the earth's granite surface and then deposited its stony debris randomly across the landscape. The big rock just sits there, its mass and weight pushing down. If a boulder prevents any green growth beneath it, so the weight of depression inhibits my neurons from forming healthy pathways to make connections of free thought, associations, and responses to stimuli. I move slowly, grindingly. Each endeavor requires more supreme effort.

One practice I have found helpful to lift the weight of my depression is to pick up things and move them. As simple as that. There have been days when simply to lift the plates and cups out of my dish rack and to place them back in the cupboard counts as a day of triumph. As I pick something up, I tell myself, "I am lifting this cup out of the rack. I have agency. I am able to accomplish this thing." It is a simple gift worthy of the Shaker hymn. I am able not to think of what weighs me down about the world or my life. I am able to witness how my brain sends signals to my arm, my hand, my back as I bend down and stand up again. I can feel my fingers on the drinking glass as I grip it and keep it from falling and breaking.

I cannot move the boulder, but I can put the dishes away. It may be a small miracle, but small miracles are still miracles. The more mindful I am of what I am doing, the more I am able to realize all of the previous miracles on which this current little miracle depends. The sand that was melted to make the glass. The house I get to live in. My spouse who still sees something in me worth loving and sharing a lifetime of meals with.

I can move this small thing even if I cannot move the massive block of depression that takes up so much space in my head. That is something.

I can move beyond my dish rack and lace up some comfortable shoes to go for a walk down the driveway or down the street. I might even get to my local Y. The hardest effort is not that actual exercise of arm curls, bench presses, or leg extensions, but simply getting there. More often than not, I stand in front of my locker at the Concord, New Hampshire YMCA and say a prayer of gratitude for having done the hard part, even before I have picked up a barbell. Getting there means I have pushed the big boulder just a fraction of a millimeter. Another miracle.

In my early twenties I lived in a foreign city, where I navigated my first long-term episode of deep depression. I was seeing a therapist, but it was before the psycho-pharmaceutical revolution that brought about Prozac and its family of selective serotonin reuptake inhibitors (SSRIs). Emotionally I was in a desperate, even dangerous place. The pain in my head was unbearable, though I could not articulate how it actually felt.

I am not sure how I survived that period of my life, except somehow I got to the local gym and decided that I had to move things. My routine of rows, pull-downs, push-ups, squat thrusts, reverse curls, and other exertions had little to do with wanting to be in shape or get physi-cally stronger, though I did notice some physical change. Becoming a "gym rat" was, somehow, more sacramental, if a sacrament is defined as "an outward and visible sign of an inward and spiritual grace." My pulling thirty, then forty kilograms toward my torso in a seated row became an outward and visible sign that God had given me the abil-ity to exert influence on an object. Over time, that set of objects—a stack of weights attached to a pulley attached to a handle—felt lighter. The sacrament of lifting weights helped me feel that other things, interior things, would budge over time, or even dissolve.

That was forty years ago.

Going to the gym is still the crucial way I keep my psychic health, especially during the long, cold, sun-starved days of a New Hampshire winter. The hardest part, still, is just getting there, which, on the surface of things, seems to be the easiest thing to do. My car is parked in the Diocesan House parking lot, two blocks from the Y. My workout clothes and sneakers are in my locker. The modest monthly membership comes out of my bank account automatically. There is hardly any obstacle at all to my going, except that darn inertia in my soul that has to consent to move from whatever may seem more important and take the short walk down the street.

Once I am there, I find familiar faces who seem to be genuinely glad to see me, though I doubt they know my name. There are people the culture sees as important: legislators, high-profile attorneys, professors, surgeons. There are people with Down syndrome exercising with new immigrants serving as trainers. And this flawed clergyman. Being greeted kindly by people is a small and colossally good thing, my depression has taught me. If mental illness brings us to the edge of the existential void, if not fully reeling into that abyss, the smile and greeting of someone who recognizes you is evidence of something good in the universe. For me, that is the presence of God.

Perhaps, then, I go to the Y in the winter for the same reasons I go to church all year round. I join others who see health, both physical and spiritual, as a good thing, a thing that makes the sacrifice of time and effort worth it. I appreciate being rewarded by seeing familiar faces, of all shapes and colors and ages and abilities, who are moving things for their health and the good of a community. The amount of weight I move and how many times I move it matter only secondarily. Once in the environment of health, the inertia of my depression gives way to movement. One push-up leads to another; one set of pull-downs leads to another. Within an hour I have asked all my muscle groups to exert influence on an inanimate object. For some reason, moving the steel, iron, or rubber plates actually shifts the weighty beast that slouches in my head. I feel better—sometimes slightly, sometimes quite significantly.

There is also something about seeing the same people so often. For sure, they, too, are engaged in some struggle. Though my introverted self rarely strikes up a conversation of my own, I sometimes overhear the conversation among fellow strivers as they pause by the bench press station or the squat rack. I hear about grandchildren struggling at school, the ugly divorce, the addiction of an adult child, the suicide of a coworker, an ailing parent moving into the dementia wing, that recalcitrant high blood pressure, or the extra ten pounds gained and lost and gained over decades. Sometimes I hear about a beautiful wedding over the weekend. I have lots to pray about as I wait for the second hand to come around during my plank, an exercise which, when done while praying, is good for both my abdominal and spiritual "core."

"Moving things" has replaced "weight lifting" in my personal lexicon of activities and practices that help me through periods of depression. "Moving things" reminds me of the glacial obstructions to my brain's neural pathways that my physical exertions somehow cause to dislodge. I commend the practice, even if it looks more like moving the pedals on a bicycle or the steps on a StairMaster, or moving your own body in a Zumba, Pilates, or yoga session. External, physical movement, however slow or slight, effects the spiritual and emotional movement that depression thwarts. If stasis feeds a depression, movement breaks the food chain, saying to the demon in the brain, "I *will*, despite your seeking to deprive me of my will."

This may sound odd, but sometimes, if I don't get to the gym, I go into the woods behind my house and move rocks. New Hampshire, like much of New England, is a place of many stone walls. I go and repair walls that appear to have no more use. The rocks are heavy. They often require a shovel, mattock, or pry bar to dislodge. I get utterly exhausted, my lungs burn from breathing hard, my hands become calloused, and my back and arms get tight. There is no earthly reason to be out there. I have been reticent to share this practice with my friends, therapist, family, or church, though my previous neighbors in Massachusetts saw the labyrinth I built among the maple and oak trees.

What called me to the rocks was the story of Jesus healing the Gerasene demoniac who was chained to the rocks and boulders in the region of the Decapolis. I meet him in the stones, where I also meet Jesus, who recognized the pain, isolation, and sadness of a man fettered by forces within him.

Moving rocks moves me into the company of the man among the tombs, as he is called in scripture, both of us freed by Jesus. I am brought at least a little closer to being in my right mind. Moving rocks is a peculiar remedy, a rather idiosyncratic form of self-medication. I don't think it will start a new movement in self-help, but who knows? I suppose I could do much worse.

I will also admit that I sometimes sense the stones speaking to me in their particularity, their primordial histories, their dust that commingles with my sweat on the muggy days when I pull them out of their cool tombs. Perhaps that's my special strain of mental illness, or my occasional brush with God's presence. A clear distinction may not be necessary or helpful. And then there's this:

> As he was now approaching the path down from the Mount of Olives, the whole multitude of the disciples began to praise God joyfully with a loud voice for all the deeds of power that they had seen, saying,

> "Blessed is the king
> who comes in the name of the Lord!

Peace in heaven,
 and glory in the highest heaven!"

Some of the Pharisees in the crowd said to
him, "Teacher, order your disciples to stop." He
answered, "I tell you, if these were silent, the stones
would shout out."

Luke 19:37–40

Some of the symptoms of depression are lack of motivation,
diminished desire, and diminished capacity to participate in
activities that bring any pleasure or satisfaction. Sometimes
it gets labeled, erroneously, as acedia or sloth, which traditional moral theologians have called a "deadly sin."

We need to be careful how we talk about sin.

When my care-less-ness comes out of a sense of cal-
lousness and hardheartedness, then I would say I am participating in sin—the willful wedge I drive between me,
God, and my neighbor. On the other hand, depression may
lead to a dispiritedness that makes it hard to care about
anything, but that is not the same. Mental illness is not a
sin. I may feel guilt or remorse, perhaps even shame, about
my lack of concern, and those feelings may prod me to say,
"Something is not right. I am disconnected from everyone,
including those I love. This does not feel like living, certainly not the life I would like to live, or at least would like
to like to live."

When my habit of carelessness is just that—a habit, a choice—to admit my disconnect is to acknowledge my sin, and may motivate me to ask for help with my habit of mind that has led me to something less than the abundant and full life God desires. When depression is the root of my isolation, those same words are a prayer for healing, much like the man of the tombs: "Jesus, have mercy on me."

Rather than feel we need to choose between sin or symptom, I find it possible, and indeed helpful, to see different angles from which to examine the pain and injury of depression. Whether my slothfulness is a sin from which I need to ask forgiveness and amendment in life, or a symptom from which I need a remedy and treatment, it hurts. It is not a life I want to live, nor the life God wants for me. If that means I take a pill, or lift a glass out of the sink, or sit in conversation with a friend or a therapist, or heave rocks in the rainy woods, I will do it. Each of these is a way out, however narrow, of the damn trap within my soul.

FOR REFLECTION AND CONVERSATION

1. How do you face the day upon waking?
2. If you are overcome by heaviness, are there strategies or activities that have helped you arise and meet the day?
3. Have there been times when the smallest daily chore is too onerous for you? How have you coped?

What happens when you have not been able to cope? How has the appearance or presence of other people helped?

4. How do you relate to the power of moving things, causing things to budge or shift? Do you see a relationship between moving things externally and feeling a shift in your spirit or soul?

5. How do you relate to the inanimate world of stones and toothbrushes? Are you more sensitive to their existence when you are depressed or in a state of pain?

PRAYER

O Jesus, you told your disciples that if they had faith the size of a mustard seed they could move mountains. My faith is smaller than the tiniest spore, and I don't need to move a mountain, I just need to move enough to help me feel better. Give me what I need to take care of my body, my mind, my soul. Get me through this day in health, moving even small things, and by the power of your Holy Spirit, move what is keeping me from knowing the joy of your presence in me. Amen.

CHAPTER EIGHT

TORMENTED

> Now the spirit of the LORD departed from Saul, and
> an evil spirit from the LORD tormented him.
>
> 1 Samuel 16:14

I do not want to share this part of myself. It is the part I probably spend the most effort and attention to make sure no one sees. But the latest eruption of violence in our nation is connected to our inability to look courageously into the most troubling parts of our souls: the place where our unexamined anger smolders, waiting for a spark to ignite a fire that could burn down the whole house. I am compelled to name my anger.

Within one week in 2019, there were three mass shootings: Gilroy, California; El Paso, Texas; and Dayton, Ohio. Each shooter was a solitary white man with enough rage in his heart to snuff out any semblance of concern or empathy for the damage he inflicted on his fellow human beings. Our elected leaders were quick to cite the "dark recesses of the internet" as the source of the mayhem. Sure. There are horrible websites that foment hate speech and physical violence. But the true danger isn't virtual.

It is time for us—especially Christians, especially Christian men, especially white Christian men—to incarnate self-examination, penitence, and amendment of life. My depression has made obvious to me that my heart contains ugliness: lust, pride, fear, rage, envy, and a tendency to take pleasure in the misfortune of others—even people I cherish. I have slammed doors. I have thrown objects. I have acted violently. I have broken glass picture frames, dented car hoods, thrown a cell phone into a black river. I have yelled obscenities in the presence of tender ears. The damage to these things is hardly worth mentioning compared to the fear I have caused in my spouse, our children, our dog.

Once, as a young priest in my first parish, I threw a chair after being criticized about some seemingly trivial thing, breaking the chair and the bookshelf it collided with. If I have come close to harming myself, it was probably less an act of despair or gloom, and more one of unbridled rage.

This is my confession and no one else's. Though I know of others—priests, bishops, and laity—who share similar stories, I will tell only my own. I am deeply humiliated by my actions. When I have found myself in a therapist's office, or in the room of a confessor, I have been blessed to be told that they are not slight things. No one has ever asked, "What did the other person do to make you feel so angry?" and given me the chance to ease my conscience by not taking responsibility. Nor has anyone said, "Oh, you mustn't be so hard on yourself. God wouldn't take these things so seriously." Thankfully, my psychiatrist and confessor, both men of faith, have never let me off so easily. Both have said, "This is serious. Pay attention to this. This is not acceptable behavior. This is not who you are meant to be."

I share my story now because I don't know how else I might better serve God's people, particularly those, like me, whose battle with depression endangers not only themselves but those around them—those closest to them and who love them. My forty-year journey with depression has taught me that "Rob just being Rob," when Rob is enraged, is not how I want to live or be.

My father was a kind, benevolent man. Mostly. But when I told him that the neighborhood bully had threatened my younger sister and me, he encouraged me to find a way to make things right by standing up and "being a man." I saved my lawn-mowing money, purchased a set of barbells from Sears, and spent a month following the Charles Atlas regime. Then, one summer evening, my sister and I went for a slow bike ride around the block by the bully's haunt. Predictably, he attacked. The reckoning is still remembered, sometimes, when I visit my hometown, and I see the victim of my revenge at the grocery store. The memory is embarrassing to me. I can see that he and I were just following the only script we, as boys, were given to address our aggression. Be a man.

The memory of my early adolescence that I much prefer to recall is riding my unicycle around the neighborhood with one of the smaller kids on my shoulders. That memory includes the "reformed" bully riding alongside me, cheering, as though we were in a parade. It brings tears of joy to my eyes, even half a century later. But I had to be reminded of that moment by my brother. I had forgotten the pure communal celebration of that evening. What I remember more keenly was the night of pinning Billy to the ground and making his face bleed. My depression brings me uncomfortably closer to the ugly sides of myself, the places Jesus seems to know, perhaps even from his own experience.

> When he had left the crowd and entered the house, his disciples asked him about the parable. He said to them, "Then do you also fail to understand? Do you not see that whatever goes into a person from outside cannot defile, since it enters, not the heart but the stomach, and goes out into the sewer?" (Thus he declared all foods clean.) And he said, "It is what comes out of a person that defiles. For it is from within, from the human heart, that evil intentions come: fornication, theft, murder, adultery,

avarice, wickedness, deceit, licentiousness, envy, slander, pride, folly. All these evil things come from within, and they defile a person."

Mark 7:17–23

There are occasions when, despite my own usually ineffective labor to be free of the tightly twisted knot of my anger, I find myself making progress. One Sunday afternoon at the Y, after a session of moving weights, I was tying my shoes in the locker room, which is reserved for men over eighteen. It is arranged by long banks of lockers. I thought I was alone; it was late and the place was soon to close.

From the other side of the row of lockers I heard the sudden angry outburst of a man shouting at himself. Actually, it sounded like he was having an argument with someone, though this other person was not physically there. Apparently, he thought he was alone as well. I could tell he was shouting at someone close to him—a spouse, a sibling, a coworker, a supervisor? I could also tell that the person who was not physically present was a woman. The man's language included words that cannot be printed here. Though I wish the reverse were true, I must admit my mouth is not entirely clean; I've dropped the occasional f-bomb. In fact, the only initials of swear words I cannot remember using might be X, Y, and Z.

But when I heard his unholy utterances, I was enraged. My space had been violated by his verbal violence. I felt like the women in my life—my spouse, my daughter, my friends and colleagues, my siblings as God's children—were being assaulted. My shoelace snapped—not a good omen for the restraint of my tongue. I reached for my clerical collar, and then decided not to put it on. I paused. I took a breath. Then another. The vile language from around the corner kept spewing.

Another breath. Then I stood up, walked around the lockers, and met a half-naked man. A startled half-naked man who realized I had heard everything.

"Really?" I said.

"What?"

"Really? You need to use language like that?"

He bristled. I wondered what would happen next.

"What's it to you? There's no one else in here. No one heard me."

"I heard you."

"And who the hell are you?"

Maybe I should have put on my collar. "I'm a husband of a woman, a father of a daughter and sons—a man who needs to say we have to do better."

"But it's a locker room."

"Yeah. I know. A locker room in the Young Men's and Women's *Christian* Association. Not that that should make any difference."

"Oh. Yeah."

"I'm not a saint here, brother. I know those words because I've used them. But, we just have to do better."

"I got sons, too," he said. "I hope they don't learn them from me."

"Thanks, man. My name's Rob, by the way." I extended my hand, feeling a little awkward shaking the hand of a man wrapped in a towel.

"I'm Jim. Nice to meet you."

"You, too. See you around." I went back to my locker to see if I could tie my shoe with half a lace.

"What the heck just happened?" I thought. That was not the "me" I knew, the "Rob who was just being Rob." Maybe it was a glimpse of the Rob who was learning to live with himself, and others, in an imperfect and maddening world. Looking back on that exchange, I wonder if Paul would have recognized in it his own strivings for God. In the same letter in which he describes God's surrender to the ways of violence as the pattern of the "mind of Christ" (Phil. 2:5), which Jesus's disciples are called to inhabit, he says:

> Not that I have already obtained this or have already reached the goal; but I press on to make it my own, because Christ Jesus has made me his own. Beloved, I do not consider that I have made it my own; but this one thing I do: forgetting what lies behind and straining forward to what lies ahead, I press on toward the goal for the prize of the heavenly call of God in Christ Jesus.
>
> Philippians 3:12–14

Well, I cannot say I can, or should, forget what lies behind. The bitter lessons of my history still instruct, still provide motivation to keep striving, to keep pressing on to the peace, the deep spiritual and emotional integration and wholeness of God that passes all understanding.

FOR REFLECTION AND CONVERSATION

1. How do you deal with anger?
2. What lessons did you learn about anger growing up?
3. How does anger feed your depression?
4. How have you learned to deal constructively with your anger?

PRAYER

O God, you know all our secrets, all our emotions and attitudes. We read in scripture of your own impatience, even of your own anger and rage. Please help me to pause and breathe and not let my anger consume me and cause pain or harm to others or myself. O Lord, as you hold within yourself all that we are and all that we feel, help us to find that deep peace that can transform all our rages into words and actions that bring new life in You. In the name of Jesus, who knows all these things about us and who loves and raises us from death to life eternal. Amen.

CHAPTER NINE

PAROCHIAL ANOREXIA

I suffered from an eating disorder in my early twenties, while I was in college. I was training to make weight for the varsity lightweight rowing team. My problem was that I was too big to be a lightweight and too small to be a heavyweight. These were the only two categories in a sport I'd come to love. Rowing allowed me to find peace in my body after fracturing my neck in a football injury as a teenager. It became my sole purpose in life; thus driven, I began to starve myself.

Standing on the scale of the first weigh-in, in mid-September of my first year of college, I weighed 170 pounds. The crew coach sighed. A freshman lightweight boat of eight rowers had to average 150 pounds each, with no one weighing more than 155. I had to lose at least 15 pounds and still be stronger than others vying for a seat on the first boat—and I had to be on the first boat. The heavyweight crew averaged more like 200 pounds. But they were big boys who were generally well over 6 feet tall and had the physiques of Atlas. If I wanted to row, I had to shrink.

So I started restricting my intake of any food. I restricted my diet to the point of absurdity. I had one piece of whole wheat toast in the morning before class. I replaced lunch with an eight-to-ten-mile run across New Hampshire's winter tundra where just staying warm required significant caloric output. I remember struggling to stay awake in my afternoon seminars. (It would actually be more accurate to say I struggled to keep from passing out.) Somehow, I summoned the drive to go to the gym or down to the docks on the Connecticut River for the team workout. Dinner was a bowl of clear soup or a large salad with some fruit and nuts mixed in. Perhaps a glass of milk, if I felt I was sufficiently abstemious.

On the days before races, when we had to step on the scale to make weight before a panel of coaches with clip-boards, I didn't even drink water. Not wanting my fellow oarsmen to have to compensate for my size, I decided that I would weigh less than the 150 average. When I stepped on the scale, I was proud when its reading told my coach and my teammates that I weighed 147—a loss of 23 pounds. Mission accomplished. Others had to put on nylon sweat suits and run a couple of miles, or strain to evacuate their bowels or bladder, and then try again. Not me. I had shrunk down to my ribcage and hipbones. My sense of suc-cess bordered on euphoria, even if the stars I saw, or the kaleidoscopic aura in my retina, was my brain trying to tell me it needed more fuel.

But the whole point of being in a varsity racing shell is to row as fast as a crew can go and compete with other crews in the hopes that you might actually win. Of course, there was the feeling of the long oar levering the boat swiftly upstream, the delight of the expansive sky with billowing clouds that gently kissed the mountains that rose out of the gentle Upper Connecticut River Valley. As Water Rat says in *The Wind in the Willows*, "Believe me, my young friend, there is nothing—absolutely nothing—half so much worth doing as simply messing about in boats."

Still, at that point of my life, I cared less about the race results than the reading on the scale. I cared less about the camaraderie than I did about winning my seat as their stroke. As my brain strained for nourishment, my appreciation of the billowing clouds, and the bright, deciduous colors of autumn, the scent of tannin and pine, all gave way to making weight. The measurement of success—races won— was replaced by pounds lost.

In the end, I lost my bearings, and my mental health. I was cranky. My days were shrouded in a kind of prickly fog. I don't know how else to describe the atmosphere in which my mind was forced to function. There were amazing people in my classes whom I didn't hang out with because socializing required an expense of energy I couldn't afford. I spent my weekend nights sequestered in the musty library stacks trying to study, but mostly falling asleep on my open copy of *Paradise Lost*. A French professor came on to me in her office during an appointment she required, and I didn't have the power to resist. I spent my first Thanksgiving away from home—forgoing my grandmother's turkey and my mother's Minnesota wild rice and mushrooms—with her in the empty college town. It was not paradise, but I was certainly lost, and too famished to realize it.

In the parable of the Prodigal Son (Luke 15:11–32), Jesus described the moment "when he came to himself. . . ." It is one of the most powerful clauses in all of scripture. We have all had moments when we were so lost that we didn't even know it. Our inner barometers of well-being became so out of sync, so inaccurate, that only a catastrophe could make us see how far we had strayed from reality. Until something jogged our awareness of ourselves, we just kept heading into a pit of destruction, or at least a pen full of pigswill.

I have led retreats where I invited participants to consider just that one clause: "but when he came to himself." Occasionally, I have encountered people who struggled to feel compassion for the young man.

"Rob, you make the words 'when he came to himself' sound like some deep spiritual, philosophical thing. He was just hungry and wanted to get a good meal. What's the big deal?"

The question always catches me by surprise. Is God not qualified to speak to a person who finds themselves facing delicate surgery, or a prisoner who finally acknowledges the results of a life lived without gratitude, or an alcoholic who finds their life out of control, or a pornography addict who realizes they have lost all capacity for true intimacy with their spouse, or an anorexic rower whose deep sense of shame manifested itself as hatred of his body?

God, somehow, broke through my wasting.

I had not been going to church. I was raised in the Episcopal Church and had found serving as an acolyte to be grounding in my otherwise anxious, acne-obsessed, adolescent life. In the transition to a college chapel, church fell between the cracks. The few times I attended the local church on campus were shrouded in a haze of self-absorption. Who were these people, all dressed in linen and tweed? They seemed to have their lives all figured out: professors, professorial spouses, deans and assorted academics, alumni fundraisers, town burghers. There were not many other students in the pews, and the few that were had an ease with talking about Jesus that I didn't share. I left church wondering how many miles I needed to run to burn off the calories of the pasty wafer and the sip of wine I had consumed in the Eucharist. Needless to say, my eucharistic theology was not very high in those days.

I came to myself—I began to see my life in Christ—in early November. I had taught myself to row in a single scull. I had taken a break from the team after my first year, finally realizing I was exhausted and burned out. But my eating habits, or more accurately, my habit of non-eating, persisted. One overcast Saturday, I took a single out on the water and rowed upstream. After an hour of gliding on the glass-like surface of the Connecticut, I was awakened out of a kind of mesmerized state, suddenly, by an awareness of a presence. It filled me. It carried me. It caused me to stop in my sliding seat and be still. I could see my breath and the steam rising from my sweaty cotton turtleneck as they mixed with the snow flurries that then disappeared on the smooth black surface of the river.

It was a silence I had not heard before, as though I had rowed into another tranquil realm that both coincided with the world in which I struggled to live and was also separate. I can't say I heard an audible voice, as Paul claimed on the Damascus road, but there was a deep and abiding presence that seemed to be *for* me; that is, it was on my side, with me and not against me. A friend and not a stranger. It was a moment like the one Jesus described when he related the story of the lost son: I came to myself, and God came to me, I now believe, introducing God's self and, in so doing, introducing my soul to me.

And I was hungry. For food. For God. For the good things God wanted for me: friends, community, love, good cheer, a joy that is deeper and more resilient than happiness.

I share this moment, one snapshot in a longer journey of recovery, because I have come to see a parallel between my mental illness at the time—bulimic exercise and restrictive anorexia—and how I have come to evaluate the health and vitality of many of our parish churches. During my parish visits, I see many, both clergy and laity, who are quite hungry for spiritual nourishment. Peter likened receiving the word of God to imbibing "pure, spiritual milk" (1 Peter 2:2). Paul told the church in Corinth that as long as they were quarreling and distracted by internal disputes, they would not be ready for solid food. Indeed, the analogy between spiritual teaching and solid food has several antecedents in scripture, going as far back as Eden and the encouragement to eat any growing thing *except* the fruit of the Tree of Knowledge of Good and Evil. The connection between our bodies' intake and our souls' well-being finds its supreme expression at the Last Supper when Jesus invited his disciples to partake of the simple meal of bread and wine.

At that table Jesus made the shocking claim that they were sharing his resurrected body and blood. The idea that "we are what we eat" comes to new meaning in the Eucharist. God enters our bodies, our guts—where the ancients located the deepest of our emotions. And God enters our minds, that unlocatable intersection between our thoughts and the perspectives of the cosmos.

My eating disorder and the downward spiral it caused in both my *psyche* (the Greek word for soul) and my body has provided me with an analogy worth exploring for our own souls and the soul of our church. We are called to consume a God who, as Moses discovered, shows up with an energy that burns without being incinerated. And yet, I have spent so many days as a priest, and now as a bishop, all but consumed with anxiety about things like average Sunday attendance, the number of children at Sunday school, the average weekly pledge, and the number of dwindling worshiping communities. It often reminds me of my Friday weigh-ins, when I agreed to the fool's covenant that bound my sense of self to a damaging body image so I could participate in a sport that was supposed to be recreational—re-creational.

Don't get me wrong. We need statistics, measurements, guideposts, and methods of assessment. When a congregation insists on paying a priest a half-time salary when the church has grown in its census and demand for teaching and pastoral care has surpassed the original letter of agreement, it helps to point to the numbers when making necessary adjustments. Likewise, numbers are hard to argue when a congregation has diminished and only a few are able to carry the burden of time and finances to keep things afloat.

The usual approach for treating eating disorders is to urge sufferers to remove all body weight scales from their living space. A counselor may also require that they cover the bathroom mirror and remove any full-length mirrors from the house, dorm, or apartment. The premise behind removing these gauges of appearance is to disarm the temptation to measure self-worth by perceived body image.

When the measurements of our well-being and health have gotten so twisted that they provide the brain with ammunition to wound itself, it is helpful, if not actually life-saving, to remove them. It took me years after my own anorexic period to recover from the constant need to burn off every calorie of food intake with some inordinate exercise. To this day I resist looking at any photograph of myself before internally checking the self-damning criticism that represents a toxic mix of pride and self-absorption that grows out of my woundedness and inability to accept the sufficiency of God's love.

I see close analogy in the church's obsession with measurements and the anorexic obsession with scales. A 2019 interview of our Presiding Bishop Michael B. Curry in the *Harvard Business Review* speaks to how the church can see numbers differently.

Average Sunday attendance at Episcopal churches has dropped by 24% in the last decade. What strategies are you using to reverse that tide?

None! Questions about church attendance and church decline are second-order questions. The first-order questions are whether we are helping our people—Episcopalians—to have living relationships with God and with other people. If the answer is yes, then issues of church growth will take care of themselves, or we'll figure out how to handle them. The first Christians—the first followers of Jesus—never had a discussion about how many people they had at church on Sunday. But they kept following Jesus and his teachings, and eventually they turned an empire upside down.[4]

The connection I am trying to show may not be immediately recognizable. What analogy can there possibly be between my long battle with a dangerous distortion of my body image as it is reflected by a bathroom scale, and the fixation on the average Sunday attendance for a local church?

The first-order questions and goals for the Church are life-giving.

- What does it look like to love and follow Jesus?
- Who is the neighbor we are called to love as ourselves?
- What is the shape of that love?
- How are we daily doing justice, loving kindness, and walking humbly with our God, which the prophet Micah told us is all God requires (Micah 6:8)?

4. Ania G. Wieckowski, "Life's Work: An Interview with Bishop Michael Curry," *Harvard Business Review*, May–June 2019, https://hbr.org/2019/05/lifes-work-an-interview-with-bishop-michael-curry.

But, in a "disordered" church, the second-order obsessions skew the perspective.

- What size is the parish budget?
- How many priests can we hire?
- What is our average attendance?

When we measure the health of our church bodies in these "trailing indicators," we find our minds set on ourselves, and our attention to the readout of the scales, rather than on the nourishment God gives us in our neighbors and in creation beyond our single-minded concern for ourselves.

This is one reason why I recently took what felt like to me as a somewhat risky tack with a parish in the diocese where I serve as bishop. A long period of some moderate but draining internal conflict and transition was inaugurated by the death of a rector whose pastorate extended for over three decades, and was followed by some predictable changes in leadership in the transition that came after. It was clear that the newly arrived rector found a congregation that was welcoming and eager to get on with God's mission in Christ. However, they were exhausted!

When I attended the vestry meeting in advance of my visitation the following week, I could see it in their faces. These are people who work hard in their vocations in the world: teachers, coaches, farmers, volunteers, business people, retirees who care for aging parents and spouses and grandchildren. As vestry members, they have been necessarily focused on the work of maintaining centuries-old buildings with eroding roofs and aging plumbing, windows that barely insulate from the New England cold and damp winters. They told me that a recent dip into their archives revealed that discussions about what to do with their expansive buildings has led to "robust conversations" (read: contentious vestry meetings) *for over thirty years.* How to balance their voracious maintenance budgets with the need to support mission, clergy, worship, and music has been at the heart of it all.

Despite all these stresses, they also see themselves in their small city as one of the respected "cardinal" parishes in our humble diocese. The church building itself was designed by the same distinguished architect of the Washington National Cathedral, the Chapels at St. Paul's School and Groton. In many ways, the building literally set in granite a body image of the church as a stable, embedded institution that serves as the immovable center point of the spiritual and moral life of the city. Increasingly over the years the responsibility to maintain that "body image," with all its attendant programs, has threatened to eclipse the original joy of the church's purpose to celebrate and worship the glory of God and to know the liberating love of Jesus.

The story of this congregation, St. Thomas, is not unique to them, of course, as many congregations who have been blessed to inherit such glorious buildings are faced with like stresses that have resulted in vestry meetings focused on strained budgets negotiating the hard choices of fixing leaking roofs and crumbling mortar on the one hand and paying clergy and staff salaries or investing in new missions on the other. Quite often the first sacrifice to be made is prayer, contemplation of the gospel, setting aside time to bear witness to the movement of God in the lives of those sitting around the table. I have come to recognize the symptoms of a spiritual anorexia with its distorting and controlling message that says, "How can we think about Jesus when we've got to first make sure the building is intact?" And so the people look exhausted, and when the bishop arrives with queries about the state of their joy or their souls, they look a bit like deer on the New Hampshire night roads, caught in the headlights, stunned into silence.

It's those moments in a vestry meeting or parish forum that have led me to say that I no longer want to be complicit in the spiritual starvation of God's people. There are days when I wish that instead of being given a wooden crosier at my ordination I was given a backhoe and a bulldozer to free my beloved people from the strain of having to preserve, and heat, buildings that no longer allow the saints to share the freedom and life promised them by a Savior who started not a campus of stately buildings, but a movement of love and relationship. But since I am without those pieces of excavation, there are other, certainly less violent, implements at our disposal.

What I found myself saying after looking into the faithful but haggard faces of this vestry is similar to what a specialist in treating an eating disorder would prescribe. An equivalent approach comes to mind. For a season, say for even a whole year, stop looking at the scale! Cover up the mirrors in which you see yourself as either being too heavy or too light. Just concentrate on the habits of health and holiness that have nourished and sustained the Christian communion for over two millennia—prayer, sacred reading of scripture, keeping of the Sabbath, visiting the sick, feeding the hungry, discerning leaders for mission and ministry. Just those things. But those things. What if at least 90 percent of a vestry meeting was taken up in sharing stories about how the parish leaders actually went to their neighbors, especially the neighbors whose political leanings may be different from theirs, in order to re-weave the social fabric, now so frayed and torn by our present cultural habits?

Admittedly, it may seem that I've veered from my topic of depression by dedicating some time to describe what I called "parochial anorexia." Here's why I feel called to do so: one of the occupational hazards of parish ministry, whether you are a devoted lay member, warden, deacon, priest, or bishop, is that the mood of a parish can so often have a direct bearing on your own state of mind. So often, too often, this is a sign of just being too close, too psychically interwoven with the parish or the church organization you serve. Of course, this emotional enmeshment doesn't just happen in religious work—my dad was a salesman, and when his sales performance was seen as dropping, or if there was ugly conflict in his office, he felt crummy and a cloud of discontent came home with him into our house. But the irony is particularly cruel when the place we go to come to know the joy of Jesus becomes instead the place of malaise, sadness, and despair.

As a bishop, I've driven away from congregations feeling some gratification that the sermon was received well, the hospitality was warm, the gospel message of the Resurrection was shared by a healthy portion of the worshiping assembly. But facing the intractable truths of the dwindling population of the village, the aging of the membership, the impending retirement of the beloved part-time priest with little prospect of finding her replacement—all these facts have made the vestry meetings after coffee hour feel hopeless, frightened, anxious, and depressed. It's just like we were facing massive boulders, which may be one reason my going into the woods with a pry bar, chains, and winches actually gives me some relief. I drive away from such meetings feeling in my heart and mind something of the burden and fret my fellow members in the church are experiencing. Yes, there is a need for healthy self-differentiation and detachment in the ministry, but to not have compassion, to *feel or suffer with*, is to lose the soulfulness of the calling to be a minister, whether lay or ordained.

Now you are the body of Christ and individually
members of it.

1 Corinthians 12:27

The metaphor of the church as the Body of Christ, one
of Paul's most central and effective images, means that we
might feel vulnerable to the depression of a congregation.
And yes, Christian congregations can undergo depressions.
Some are short-lived. Others have gone on for years, even
generations. Sometimes when the parish is depressed for
a prolonged period, its members can suffer a similar diagnosis. I wonder if part of my role as a bishop, particularly
as a bishop who knows depression, is to recognize it when
I see it in a congregation and to find ways to care and treat
the soul of the parish by recalling it to practices that lead,
if not to glee or happiness, then to the joy that empowers
us to share the suffering of a community in the abiding love
of God.

FOR REFLECTION AND CONVERSATION

1. What are the physical manifestations or symptoms of
    your depression?
2. Are there habits of mind and body that you have
    adopted that may have seemed good and healthy at
    one time in your life but now lead you to a place of
    dis-ease and despair?

3. What are the measures of your joy?
4. Have you measured yourself, physically or emotionally, by unrealistic comparisons with others?
5. Can you allow yourself to be "right-sized" as God has called you to be, or do you feel you need to fit into a box of expectations that have been imposed by someone else? How are those expectations measured?

PRAYER

O God, you see us as we really are, all the ways we seem to measure up and all the ways we disappoint, and by your grace you love us nonetheless. Help us to see ourselves as you might see us, beautiful and broken, bold and afraid, and then help us to love each other, our neighbors and ourselves, as you love us, you who are the source of all love. In the name of the crucified and risen Jesus Christ. Amen.

CHAPTER TEN

Opening the Mind

One thing that I have found helpful, as I have worked to move from the self-centeredness of depression to engaging with the world outside my own thoughts and feelings, is the practice of mindfulness. I acknowledge the potential objections to the phrase "self-centeredness of depression." I do not mean to suggest that depression is the result of selfishness, or reduce it to being overly concerned with one's own self to the exclusion of the larger community. One definition of depression is "anger turned inward." It's the "turned inward" part that I am working to name.

I don't mean that a person living with depression is a narcissist, or utterly preoccupied with the preservation of the self. However, I have noticed that when I am in the depths of a depressive period, I would rather curl up in a fetal position than go out and be sociable, or be curious about the lives of others, or feel empathy. I am consumed with myself, absorbed with myself. I can't see beyond me.

My depression often feels like my soul is trying to protect itself from any kind of threat, including the threats that others may be facing. Compassion costs. And yet its opposite, isolation, is toxic.

Jane Hirshfield wrote a poem called "Happiness" that looks at the life of Francis of Assisi as the model of mindfulness, of being so empathic with all living things, from a wolf, fierce and hungry, to fearless birds who reputedly preached to him, to the amoeba and the plankton about to be swallowed by the skein of a whale's mouth. Even the shapeless other entities, so often seen as foes, are described as companions to the saint.

> Hopelessness, Desperateness, Loneliness,
> even the fire-tongued Anger . . .

The way to happiness, Hirshfield suggests, is not by closing oneself off from the community of beings and things, but by becoming "porous, opened, rinsed through" by and with them.

Galway Kinnell's short poem "Prayer" also emanates from a place of mindful vulnerability to what life dishes out, whatever it dishes out.

> Whatever happens. Whatever
> *what is* is what I want.
> Only that. But that.

How can we practice in order to enter into that space of invulnerable vulnerability, to feel all the joy and sorrow, the hilarity and the utter tragedy of our world, and still remain standing, and still keep our souls somehow intact and whole? How can we remain porous, opened, rinsed through, to the opulent Other that is *what is*? The repetition of the word *is* recalls the theophany of God on the holy mountain of the burning bush when God revealed the divine identity as I AM: that is, Being itself. Though it often terrifies me as much as it comforts me, this is all I want, too. *But that.*

The first practice of mindfulness is prayer. Even wordless prayer—becoming comfortable in the silence that is the foundation of all authentic relationships. Perhaps it begins with five minutes alone in a room, or with others. For some, that time may feel like an eternity at first, but over time, a short period of quiet will become like an appetizer, something that makes you realize how hungry you are; something that spurs a hunger for more.

Without silence in my day, several times in my day, I can feel disoriented, disconnected from the stirrings in my heart. I need sufficient and robust quiet to allow my soul the chance to know how it is responding to words or images or news. Otherwise, my mind is too crowded, too saturated. A period of silence allows the sponge of my soul to be wrung out so that I can take in the next thing. Like breathing, silence allows me to exhale what I have taken in but cannot keep lest I am contaminated by what is harmful and noxious.

By silence, I do not mean the absence of sound or noise. To find a place completely devoid of sound is virtually impossible in our world. Probably, the absence of sound can only be found in some artificial setting, such as a recording studio with soundproofed surfaces whose purpose is not to eliminate sound, but to distill the sound of the musician whose music the room awaits. Silence, in mindful meditation or centering prayer, allows for the sounds that surround us all the time.

The water I hear dripping in the cellar where I am writing, the neighbor's car starting, the low buzz of the hummingbird approaching the feeder outside the window, a child's footfall upstairs. A jet plane a mile above. A honk. Even a distant gunshot. All these are sounds I hear as I practice silence. They represent what *is*. As such, they allow me to be more like the amoeba in Hirshfield's poem, "touched on all sides by the opulent Other," who is the I AM. Allowing myself to witness and notice the sounds, without pondering their meaning or reasons for being, grants me the chance to be less self-focused, less in my own toxic, enclosed and gated self, and more able to see myself as part of a universe that exists beyond me and still allows me, even now wants me, to live.

There is a time-honored tradition of pilgrimage, or traveling to certain sacred sites where parts of the story of our spiritual tradition took place. The myriad sites in what we often call the Holy Land—Palestine and Israel—come to mind. The routes of Paul in his travels in Asia Minor and the Mediterranean. Pilgrimages go to where the relics of saints have found their permanent rest, where a spiritual traveler can pause and find themselves in the presence of one who came to know and bear witness to the Presence who is God, even when that witness cost them their very life. That desire to be drawn closer is what leads many to walk the Camino de Santiago de Compostela in Spain, or St. Cuthbert's Way in England, to name two.

A few years ago, my spouse and I joined hundreds of other pilgrims in Hayneville, Alabama, to visit the site of the martyrdom of Jonathan Daniels, a person of deep importance in New Hampshire whose writings and slaying at the hands of a white supremacist during the Civil Rights movement led him to be venerated not only in the Granite State, but at the Washington National Cathedral and even in Canterbury.

In my desire to walk out of my depression, I have been more often inclined to go on pilgrimage in the "holy land" that is closer to home: the nature that surrounds where I am blessed to live, work, and play. I am not the only one. Many churches are coming again to see the evangelical power of walking in nature as a way of inviting their own members, as well as those who may describe themselves as "religiously homeless" or "spiritual but not religious," to take walks in woods, mountains, meadows, and deserts. We hear reports of "Holy Hikes" in California, and "Sacred Saunters" along portions of the Appalachian Trail in Central Pennsylvania. The word "saunter" has a fascinating etymology. When pilgrims from Western Europe were asked where they were going, the reply in French was to the Sante Terre, the Holy Land. Over time, Sante Terre became the verb "to saunter." I cannot count the times when, uninspired and unmotivated to undertake any kind of more rigorous exercise, but knowing that my soul would benefit from lungs full of fresh air, fields of green things, and the music of the wind through branches and the gurgling streams, I have simply sauntered in a back field or a city park, stopping when I needed to watch a bird or notice a troubling thought move on like a passing cloud. All land can be holy, a place where God's Spirit can shift a soul toward a deep peace and restored wholeness, a *shalom.*

One such pilgrimage actually involved as much water as it did land. In the summer of 2017, the Episcopal Church's New England diocese, which we call Province One, organized a forty-day and forty-night "River of Life" pilgrimage. Several dozen people of all ages paddled by canoe or kayak from the source of the Connecticut River at the border of New Hampshire and Quebec to its estuarial emptying on the Connecticut shoreline close to where Long Island Sound meets the Atlantic Ocean. The project involved careful planning for the safety and care of the pilgrims, who needed food, safe directions, and shelter from passing storms and floods. It was not an adventure trip, as one might find advertised in a glossy magazine like *Outdoor.* Rather, it was a journey of prayer, of keeping vigil, of slow movement—except for the flood stage we encountered near Hartford after a torrential rain drastically increased the river's volume for a couple of days.

Each day began with a silent breakfast around a campfire, readings from a devotional manual compiled by our leaders for the pilgrimage, and then at least two hours of intentional silence on the river with nothing but the sound of our paddles entering and exiting the waters. The absence of words made us more attuned to the wildness around us—wind, water, loons, eagles, terns, osprey—as well as the wildness of our heartbeats and breathing, the movement of our bodies through space and time, and the miracle of that movement. I was reminded of what Ishmael says in the opening paragraph of *Moby Dick*: "Yes, as everyone knows, meditation and water are wedded forever."

For several of the participants, including at least a couple bishops, it was an experience of mindful movement in God's presence that led to a change of mind about life and ministry. The Greek word for a change of mind or heart is *metanoia.* We were taught in church that the word means not only "repentance," but "a radical change of mind." My experience on the water with my fellow paddlers was not only a change of mind, but an opening. The pictures of me during that time on the water show a bearded man who is clearly at one with himself, his companions, and God's creation, even in the moment when we had to get off the water quickly because of a severe thunderstorm over Vermont's Mount Ascutney that threatened to unleash its lightning and rain. We pulled our vessels off the river and gathered at the edge of a farmer's field. Our guides told us to stand on our life vests so that if and when lightning struck, we would be insulated from any electrical charge that might travel through the wet ground.

We stood in a semicircle, in silence, watching the lightning strike the mountainside and come down into the valley. *We might soon be goners*, I thought. But as we stood, drenched by a summer rain and feeling the chill of the evening, some of us shivering either from the cold or the intense uncertainty, I looked around and I saw smiles. Warmth in the eyes of my fellow pilgrims. I felt within myself a kind of cheerfulness. On the cusp of a possible catastrophe, there was something of Kinnell's prayer: "Whatever happens is what I want."

I hear echoes of Jesus's prayer in the Garden of Gethsemane in those words. In the middle of the agony just before his arrest and then crucifixion, Jesus trusted the promise of glory after his death. He was simultaneously vulnerable and invulnerable, confident of the destiny that was his from before the beginning of Creation. This is at the very heart of my understanding of the Christian faith: being bound to Christ's death and resurrection, we get to share the glory of God, notwithstanding the suffering of the present time. The saints lived their lives steeped in that knowledge, as did the martyrs of the faith. Dietrich Bonhoeffer prepared for his own hanging at the hands of the Nazis, stating that his death would be both end and "for me, the beginning."

On occasion I am called to stand, or walk, in solidarity with the oppressed, the vulnerable, and the peacemakers. Marching alongside hundreds of others at a Black Lives Matter march in Manchester, New Hampshire, was its own pilgrimage of faith. We saw several white men carrying military-style semi-automatic rifles and lining our route. New Hampshire is a state that allows its citizens to carry their weapons unconcealed. The armed men were there not to show their grief at the deaths of unarmed black men who have lost their lives in police actions. Instead, they stood on the sidewalks purely to intimidate and show their anger at the marchers.

The day after the march, I received a piece of anonymous mail, marked with a swastika, expressing deep disgust with me. I recognize how protected and insulated my life has been from such threats and expressions of hatred. The road has not been stony, the rod not chastening or bitter for folks like me: white, straight, male, middle class, born in the soft enclaves of American suburbia. My initial response to such threats is to retreat. My depression can make me more prone to protect myself and to burrow. I want to withdraw, from engagement, from speaking, from offering witness, from pilgrimage.

The memory of standing in a lightning storm, drenched in a chilling summer downpour, thrashed by winds, and among friends standing ready to meet whatever happened with grace and courage—even joy—serves as a response to my frail and faltering faith. Being porous, drenched in reality. I think that is what Jesus spoke of when he said, "I have said these things to you so that my joy may be in you, and that your joy may be complete" (John 15:11).

And he said it on the night before his execution.

That's the joy I want, for myself and the world. Only that. But that.

Friendship is another practice of walking together through life—the interactive practice of "opening" ourselves to the healing we need from being trapped within our own swirl of toxic thoughts. Dixon Chibanda is one of only twelve psychiatrists in all of Zimbabwe, a nation of over sixteen million. In sub-Saharan Africa, the ratio of mental health professionals to the population is one to 1.5 million. Chibanda, a psychiatrist in Harare, despaired at the staggering numbers of Zimbabweans living with depression and at the high rates of suicide in the wake of poverty, the prevalence of HIV/AIDS, drug addiction, and the aftermath of a brutal civil war.

The root causes of depression, despair, and hopelessness are loneliness and isolation, whether in Zimbabwe or America. Common sense and experience tell us that addressing loneliness is a step toward healing depression and preventing suicide. Chibanda realized his country had a huge resource in the willingness and availability of elder women—the grandmothers—even in the most remote villages. He and his team set up "Friendship Benches" all across the country.

Since 2006, they have trained over four hundred grandmothers to sit and listen for free in more than seventy communities across the country. In 2017 alone, the Friendship Benches helped over thirty thousand people. These elderly women have survived generations of hardship, including the Rhodesian Bush War, the Matabeleland massacre, and other atrocities. They are available to listen to anyone who approaches. They are trained in basic skills of talk therapy without using clinical terms like "suicidal ideation" or even "depression." They communicate through culturally rooted concepts that people can identify with. The Shona word for depression is *kufungisisa,* literally "thinking too much." Alongside their formal training, they have incorporated Shona concepts of *kuvhura pfungwa*—opening up the mind and strengthening the spirit.[5]

---

5. Rachel Nuwer, "How a Bench and a Team of Grandmothers Can Tackle Depression," BBC, October 16, 2018, Future, http:// www.bbc.com/future/story/20181015-how-one-bench-and-a-team -of-grandmothers-can-beat-depression.

Learning about the Friendship Benches lifted my heart at the simple power of friendship among strangers. As a bishop, I wonder how our churches might better be friendship benches for those scores of people in our communities burdened with depression, with "thinking too much." As one who understands *kufungisisa*, even though I don't speak Shona, I am grateful for the "grandmothers" in my life who have opened my mind with their listening hearts.

For Reflection and Conversation

1. What does the word "mindfulness" mean to you?
2. How do you understand the connection between mindfulness and prayer? What are the differences?
3. Where are the friendship benches in your life?
4. To what extent have our churches succeeded and failed to be friendship benches for those scores of people in our communities so burdened by political rancor, poverty, lack of opportunity, domestic and gun violence, and addiction?

Prayer

Most Holy Trinity, you are a God of fellowship, of communion, of trust, of with-ness. Help me when I become convinced that I am in this life all alone. Help me not be afraid or ashamed to reach out to friends and companions, doctors, therapists, all those who are ready and eager to talk with me when I am in crisis. For it is through our being together that we come to know the closeness of your love and your healing and your life-giving presence, in the name of the Father and the Son and the Holy Spirit. Amen.

LIVING IN THE REALM
OF NONETHELESS

To end, I would like to share the beginning of this journey. I remember a cold, damp, and starless November
night. I was standing in the yard of our house. My wife
and two young children were inside setting the table for
supper, and I could hear their singing some bright Beatles
song like "Twist and Shout" and laughing. The glow of the
kitchen lights spilled out into the misty night air. I had just
come back from a short run after my day as the Episcopal
chaplain at the University of Connecticut and pastor of a
parish in that college town. It was a great first job for a
newly ordained minister, providing me ample opportunity
to be a part of a community that seemed to appreciate
who I was. My wife and I had two amazing children, and
it was possible a third was on the way. My whole life—all
of my upbringing, my education as an English major with

philosophical leanings, even growing up in an imperfect home tinged with alcoholism and a little abuse—felt like it could integrate into my life as priest.

I remember lying down in the frosted fall grass and noticing the steam from my breath and sweat rising up from my body into the dark. And I thought, "Okay. I have no more desire, except to die. I wish I could evaporate and just disappear. I wish I could dissolve right here and not even leave an impression in this grass." And I was surprised.

I don't remember getting up, but I must have. I must have joined my family, joined the laughter, listened to stories about school and my wife's day at her work. A few days later, I started coughing uncontrollably, got a fever, and could barely move. At the parish secretary's urging I went to the doctor, who noticed that there was something else going on besides my infected lungs. He asked me some questions: Are you eating? Are you sleeping well? Do you have any libido? Everything was a big no.

Does your family find you irritable? Are you moody? Have you had thoughts about harming yourself or ending your life? All yes. I told him about my wish to evaporate on the lawn, but I didn't tell him about the oak tree that seemed perfectly positioned for my speeding Subaru on a particular curve on Codfish Falls Road and how it sometimes called to me like the Sirens called to Odysseus.

He said, "My friend, you're really sick. You've got pneumonia. But we can fix that. I'm more worried about your depression. It is real and nothing to shrug off. In fact, you can't shrug it off. I'm going to give you something for it, but I want you to talk to someone I know. Let me be clear, this depression is more a threat to your life than your pneumonia."

That was over twenty-five years ago. Though I'm not with the same therapist the doctor recommended, I have been seeing Dr. Schwartz now for almost that long. I remember the first time he saw me.

"You're very sick," he said, and then some talk about psychodynamic therapy, Freud, medicine. All I heard was, "You're very sick," and "This is serious." Then he handed me a card with his cell phone number. "And here's the thing, my treatment only works *if you're alive.* You call me if you find yourself wanting to leave us."

At that moment, I was stunned into the truth that I was in the throes of a disease I couldn't fix on my own. The risk of catastrophe for those whom I loved and who loved me—not to mention for myself—was high. And better mental health was not something I could attain by my own lone striving.

As a bishop, these pages represent a "coming out" for me: coming out of the closet of mental illness. When I shared my thought of revealing my struggle with depression, my table of five cherished colleagues in the House of Bishops tenderly quipped that "coming out" might become a kind of tradition for Episcopal bishops in New Hampshire. My predecessor, Gene Robinson, who was consecrated in 2003, was the first openly gay man to be made a bishop in the Christian church.

One of those at my table gently jibed that I could say, "I'm not gay. I'm depressed!" Humor can salve.

It still feels like a surprise to me that I've been entrusted with this work of leading not only a tiny church, but a whole diocese of God's children into lives of hope, community, purpose, and life when I know so much of the other side of these things: despair, isolation, the meaningless abyss, even death. Somehow, I have been lucky; perhaps the better word is "privileged." I've had a talented team of a therapist, a coach, and a spiritual director. I'm like a NASCAR driver with a whole crew so that when I'm in the pit that the Psalmist often refers to, I have people I can call to get what I need to keep going. Not everyone has this crew. Actually, few do, which is plainly and cruelly unjust. As I write this I am aware of no fewer than five people within a fifteen-mile radius of my house who have taken their own lives in the past two weeks, ranging in age from nineteen to seventy years old.

The popular belief is that religious people, especially Christians and certainly church leaders, are supposed to be about happiness, rejoicing, celebration, hope, love, and light. The fact is that we clergy are called into some of the most vulnerable spaces of our communities. We hear stories of addiction, abuse, violence, and crime, some of them heinous. We counsel both saints and sinners. We bury loved ones, and we bury despised ones. We join families whose young children are dying of myriad kinds of disease or trauma. And we do all these things when we have our own families and marriages, which look more like a Hieronymus Bosch tableau than a *Saturday Evening Post* cover scene by Norman Rockwell.

But I continue to learn to live with my mental illness, and the emphasis is on the phrase *live with*: not in denial or rejection of it, but with it. I have shared my story with as much honesty and compassion as I can muster, hoping to accompany others on that same journey.

I want to go back to the maple tree I mentioned that subsumed the stretch of rusted barbed wire into its vascular pith over time. Cell by cell, the tree came to accept and integrate the source of its irritation and suffering. And the tree has flourished in spite of the thorny wire. The leaves were brilliant, almost incandescently red this year. In the spring, I tapped the trunk and drew buckets of sap with no risk of harm to the tree. That's the story of suffering, even of my own suffering, that I want to tell. It seems trite to call the tree happy or gleeful, yet my soul is convinced of the arbor's participation in the infinitely more robust and enduring joy found at the heart of God's Presence.

> Let the heavens be glad, and let the earth rejoice;
>> let the sea roar, and all that fills it;
>> let the field exult, and everything in it.
> Then shall all the trees of the forest sing for joy
>> before the LORD; for he is coming,
>> for he is coming to judge the earth.
>
> Psalm 96:11–13

That note of God's judgment is not to be ignored. We know many persons who reject religious faith or affiliation because any notion of judgment seems opposed to love and life. "Who are you or I to judge my or anyone else's behavior?" is presented as a commonplace and quick position against any expression of organized or institutional religion. Judgment and joy are seen as opposed to one another. But the note of God's impending reckoning stands as a salutary corrective to any shallow giddiness or glee we might be tempted to equate with Christian belief. Our Lord returns to life and leaves the tomb still bearing the wounds of the nails and the lance. Easter morning somehow gives us the resilience and power to remember what happens on Good Friday.

Likewise, my friend the tree in the woods, the sugar maple with the ingested rusted barbed wire, calls to mind those many barbs that are all now wounding our souls. Here I am speaking of those obnoxious distresses that irritate and afflict any of us who are awake in this present age. Allow me to name just a few of the barbs that press on us: the rise in expression of white supremacist and white nationalist rhetoric and policies that threaten to poison efforts to repair the ravages of racism, slavery, and genocide; the steady choking of the planet's capacity to absorb greenhouse gases and the potential mass extinction caused by climate change; the widening and obscene disparity of opportunity and wealth in almost every nation; and the heightened threat of a return to an economically and morally bankrupting arms race of weapons of mass destruction.

Any one of these crises can both cause one to despair and further fuel a predisposition to depression and anxiety. More and more is being written about the emotional and psychic costs of "white fragility" or "eco-grief." It may be a matter of time before such phrases make their way into the bible for mental health professionals, the massive *Diagnostic and Statistical Manual of Mental Disorders (DSM-5)* published by the American Psychiatric Association. Considering the enormity of these ecological, social, economic, and political crises, and how seemingly feeble any one individual's power is to lessen their deleterious effects, I wonder if the post–World War II age, once famously described by W.H. Auden as "the Age of Anxiety," might be giving way to an "Age of Apocalyptic Despair."

Learning to *live* with depression has been a process of learning how to dwell with a modicum of peace in the realms of the *nevertheless,* the *notwithstanding,* and the *despite all this.* Yes. It is true that I am an isolated, lonely, utterly limited, and insignificant speck of dust on this planet, in this universe. This is at least part of the cold truth that my sorry face gets rubbed in every Ash Wednesday: remember that you are dust and to dust you shall return.

And yes, it is also true that God continues to work with dust, with ashes, with the mud of the primordial ooze, even with the messes of our own making. Along with at least a few other depressed friends of mine, I find Ash Wednesday to be a day of tremendous hope and even joy. It's when God says to me, "I know who you are. We get to start it all anew, as though for the first time. I will never, ever tire of re-creating you into the one I love. Never."

It has taken decades of prayer, hundreds of days of staring blankly into space or through grimy windows, numerous intervals of kneeling on slate church floors, frequent chats over more coffee than any body should healthfully process, several medications, more prayer, countless hours of talk therapy with all their awkward silences and bumbling attempts to understand why I am who I am and how my particular, peculiar stretch of barbed wire came to get inside of me. More recently, I have discovered a source of compassion with myself and with others who are feeling so despondent about their lives and the way things look in our world. One sufferer of mental illness told me that having the opportunity to tell the story among others in her church of her own struggle was more enlivening and liberating than years of private therapy. I suspect strongly that the sense of acceptance and freedom she felt was the result of both the arduous individual therapy *and* the discovery that those she thought would dismiss or belittle her were actually her friends, perhaps even fellow sojourners on the road to health.

As for the crippling sense that we are powerless to mend the tears in our ecological and social fabric—certainly there are not many fabrics that bind us to God, the Creation, and each other, but one—I find hope in some of the church's most ancient teaching. Origen, certainly a complicated thinker of third-century BCE Alexandria, proclaimed a belief that as children of God, each of us, every one of us, is of infinite value in God's realm. Indeed, within us is a microcosm, a little universe, reflecting and in intimate communion with God. Each of us is a little church, the entire Body of Christ, even as we remain just a member of that Body. We find ourselves in our relationship with the whole: "You yourself are even another little world and have within you the sun and the moon and also the stars."

Whenever I am able to muster kindness, compassion, a ray of light, however dim, for just one other person, even if that one person is at first myself, then there is God. This truth is borne out by the scores of reliable healings, feedings, and raising of Jesus, who did so much with such tiny offerings: a touch of spittle-covered fingers, a blessing of a few loaves and a couple of fish, a word, a gaze out of which spilled a universe of God's love. I am certain that the fierce adhesion of sin makes it impossible that any one of us, or even a whole movement of fallen humans, will on their own save the planet, repair the breaches of oppression and violence in our world. I have little hope in humankind working on its own, which is why I have come to believe in the power of God's grace, working within us, even *in spite of ourselves.* I find this truth not a source of mental illness or despair, but the ground out of which life, hope, light springs.

Today I walked once more past that sugar maple tree and looked at it carefully again. I noticed just how deep the steel wire is embedded. In fact, in a knothole within the bark, I noticed a little space where a bird had left some hay and straw for the beginnings of a nest. And guarding her tiny home was wire, at least three inches embedded in the tree, and in the perfect shape of a cross.

This book is meant to be like that tree, a companion that others will lean on in those times of desperate isolation and pain. I have learned to live with depression, and I pray every day for those whose struggle will end in harm or death. I know enough of what it is like to so suffer to prevent me from feeling anything but compassion and sorrow.

I've got something like barbed wire in my soul. It sometimes makes me depressed. I see it in others, and I am so deeply honored when they feel they can tell me of their own struggle to learn to live with this damn condition. I am still alive.

I ache for you to be alive, too.
Hold on.
The woods can truly be lovely, even if dark and deep.
Hold on.
For God's sake, for mine,
for this world's sake, and for yours,
hold on.

RESOURCES

I solation is depression's preferred fuel, the fumes of which are cruel and toxic. I have found these practices and resources to help me re-weave, thread by thread, my soul's torn fabric. Daily reading of scripture and prayer has been a way of connecting with so many in the church's communion around the world. Often I just read alone from one of my tattered two-volume editions of the Daily Office; anyone with a Bible can follow the same schedule of readings found in the lectionary section of the Book of Common Prayer. There have been days when my energy has been so limited that I've just logged on to missionstclare.com and allowed the whole brief prayer service to be audibly read to me. At Diocesan House in New Hampshire, our staff has gotten into the practice of gathering for noonday prayers every day and reading selections from the Office. The practice of praying together, extemporaneously, as a staff has had a positive, buoying effect, not only on Diocesan House, but, mysteriously, on the spirit of the whole diocese.

There are more condensed and easily accessible ways of maintaining a spiritual and emotional grounding in the wider church's witness of scripture: Forward Movement's Day by Day pamphlets have been a staple for countless sinners and saints, as necessary as anything to get through a day. I know this because as a parish priest I remember how we once forgot to renew the church's subscription to the quarterly shipment of booklets made available to our congregation. The irate phone calls and e-mails that followed were a statement of how necessary the daily Bible verse and the accompanying meditations had become to the psychic health of our community.

In recent years the phenomenon of mindfulness meditation has taken root. This is an ancient practice of deliberately "opening the mind," described earlier in this book, and of learning a deep peace that is more robust and durable than what life throws at us. Practices of mindful attention to one's breath, heartbeat, a word from scripture, or a repeated brief prayer have provided me, and countless others, with a path through some very rugged terrain. Though the new interest in mindful meditation, or insight meditation, may have its roots in Eastern, non-Christian traditions, there is plenty of evidence of the helpful benefits of interfaith interaction. The *Ego Eimi* practice I shared previously obviously owes much to these interactions and dialogues. A website that offers more about Christian-Buddhist dialogue and explores how meditation on the Gospel can be deepened by mindfulness is Dr. Robert A. Jonas's work at the Empty Bell, www.emptybell.org.

It should be stated, as I have shared in the chapter titled "Tormented," that those afflicted with depression are not the only ones who suffer from its effects. Spouses, family, loved ones, and friends can often be perplexed by our withdrawal, irritability, or self-medicating behaviors. The depressed one is usually not adequately able to coach or reassure those in the orbit of their suffering. For our friends and family I highly recommend two books: *What To Do When Someone You Love Is Depressed,* by Mitch and Susan Golant (Henry Holt and Co., 2007), and *When Someone You Love Is Depressed: How to Help Your Loved One Without Losing Yourself,* by Laura Epstein Rosen and Xavier Francisco Amador (Fireside Simon & Schuster, 1997).

As has been said, being a person of faith or being a religious leader does not make anyone immune from mental illness. However, the lingering stigma about mental illness often diminishes our willingness to share our stories and to seek appropriate help. I have been very grateful for the Rev. Dr. Kathryn Greene-McCreight's book disclosing her own struggles with bipolar disorder. Her book *Darkness Is My Only Companion: A Christian Response to Mental Illness* (Brazos-Baker Books, 2015) is poignantly and faithfully written, and in many ways gave me the courage to share my own experience.

The National Alliance of Mental Illness (NAMI) recognizes the important role spirituality has in supporting those affected by mental illness. The Alliance is working to establish a network of congregations, clergy, and religious leaders across denominations and faiths through NAMI FaithNet, www.nami.org/NAMIFaithnet.

ACKNOWLEDGMENTS

I have felt that comfort, that "together strength" of Jesus, in the witness of countless persons who have encouraged, supported, and inspired me on this journey of writing about my depression.

I have been abundantly blessed by a team of helpers and guardians over the years, my "pit crew" who have helped me keep the wheels on: Dr. Harold Schwartz of the Institute for Living at Hartford Hospital, Brother James Koester of the Society of St. John the Evangelist, and the Rev. Mark K. J. Robinson.

Mr. Craig Kramer, whose own family's struggles and crises have resulted in his courageous leadership in the global effort of the Johnson & Johnson Corporation to "change the world's mind about mental illness."

My friend and occasional hiking partner Dr. John Aney, who, along with Dr. Schwartz, helped me to be able to write about what is known and what is still not known about the neuroscience of depression.

The Rev. Dr. Bill Harkin, priest, teacher, therapist, whom I met at a recent CREDO conference for bishops, and who was easy to befriend and lean on for encouragement in the strenuous work of writing about depression.

My friend and coach David Rynick, whose trust in the infallibility of Truth has often exceeded my own trust in it.

My colleagues and staff at the Diocesan House of the Episcopal Church of New Hampshire: Hannah Anderson, Kevin Nichols, Tina Pickering, Lynn Eaton, Gail Avery, Benge Ambrogi, Gloria Gallant, Jessi Quinn. You have heard—and tolerated—my sighs. We have labored strenuously in God's pasture in the rocky soil of New England. You have allowed me space and attention to get this word out.

This book would not have been possible without the able editing and encouragement of Milton Brasher-Cunningham. He has helped me turn sighs into words.

Nor would much be possible for me to pursue or accomplish without the resilient nourishment and forbearance of my beloved spouse of thirty years, Polly Ingraham, who, along with our fascinating children, has lived through all this with a steadfast love that must be of God.

Christians often feel that their experience of depression or mental illness is a reflection of a deficit in their faith. As a result of seeing depression as a moral shortcoming or spiritual failure, we risk more damage to ourselves and even hurt those around us by denying what is really going on. *With Sighs Too Deep for Words*, with its prayers and practical suggestions for spiritual and creative practices and resilience, is a companion for those who suffer so that they may know more deeply the resilient love of Jesus.

"*With Sighs Too Deep for Words* originates in the author's revelation of the personal secret of depression. The woods, rocks, soil, and rivers of New England are the harsh and riveting landscape where he explores suffering and beauty, pain and gift. This book is an exercise of courage and sacrifice, an offering for which I and many, many others will be immensely grateful."

— **The Very Rev. Cynthia Briggs Kittredge**
Dean and President, Seminary of the Southwest

"What a relief to hear a church leader—an Episcopal bishop, no less—tracing without shame his long struggle with depression. Weaving poetry, art, biblical passages, and his own poignant prayers, he offers inventive ways of approaching melancholy. . . . An elegantly written testament to the power of transformation through beauty and faith."

— **Christine Hemp**
author of *Wild Ride Home: Love, Loss, and a Little White Horse, a Family Memoir*

"In powerful verse, humble stories, and heartfelt prayers, Rob lets us in on his experience of living with depression. In doing so he offers life: life for himself, life for his readers, life for all who live with mental illness. This is a story of ongoing resurrection."

— **The Rt. Rev. Ian T. Douglas**
Bishop of the Episcopal Church in Connecticut

Since 2012, **A. Robert Hirschfeld** has served as the Tenth Bishop of the Episcopal Church of New Hampshire. He is also an artist and sculler.

CHURCH PUBLISHING INCORPORATED

www.churchpublishing.org/withsighstoodeepforwords
Available as an ebook

ISBN 978-1-64065-260-6

9 781640 652606 >